TANSTAAFL*

---

* There ain't no such thing as a free lunch

Edwin G. Dolan
Dartmouth College

HOLT, RINEHART AND WINSTON, INC.
NEW YORK   CHICAGO   SAN FRANCISCO   ATLANTA
DALLAS   MONTREAL   TORONTO   LONDON   SYDNEY

TANSTAAFL*

THE ECONOMIC STRATEGY FOR
ENVIRONMENTAL CRISIS

* There ain't no such thing as a free lunch

Excerpts from *The Economy of Cities,* by Jane Jacobs on p. 107 copyright © 1969 by Jane Jacobs. Reprinted by permission of Random House, Inc.

ILLUSTRATED BY FRANK C. SMITH
COVER PHOTOGRAPH BY JOHN KING

preface

The original impetus for this book came in the form of an invitation to speak on the subject of economics and the environment at the Royalton College Summer Institute for Social Studies, held in July 1970 at South Royalton, Vermont. As I began to prepare for this seminar it became clear to me that the topic had a dual aspect. On the one hand I found myself formulating an ecological critique of economics. The discipline of economics is traditionally devoted to the study of how scarce resources can best be allocated to fulfill unlimited and competing human desires. In the past it has exhibited a disturbing tendency to overlook or belittle the inefficiencies and irrationalities in resource use arising from the circular interdependence of man, the producer, with his natural environment. This "science of scarcity" has ironically failed to recognize the scarcity of many natural resources, especially those involved in the disposal of wastes, and has consequently failed to account fully for the costs of production and consumption. Many economic policies, long thought conducive to the improvement of material welfare, clearly need a thorough reexamination in the light of ecological considerations.

On the other hand it became apparent to me that a distressingly large number of writers responsible for bringing the environmental crisis to the center of public attention were as ignorant of the most elementary principles of economics as economists were of ecology. A variety of naïve and ill-considered policies for coping with the crisis were put into circulation which, if implemented, would at best achieve their desired environmental objectives only at the expense of wastefully large economic sacrifices, and at worst would perpetuate in an altered but no less pernicious form the very evils they were intended to combat.

I concluded that unless an ecological consciousness could be introduced into economics, and unless the emotionalism and mythology of the popular environmental literature could be supplemented by reasoned analysis, the wave of ecological enthusiasm which had crested with the celebration of Earth Day in April 1970 would recede without lasting effect.

I therefore address this book to concerned laymen, students, and professionals in the hope that it will help channel thought and discussion toward the development of a genuine science of ecological economics.

I would like to thank Dr. Anthony N. Doria, President of Royalton College, for extending the original invitation to speak at the Summer Institute for Social Studies; and to thank my colleagues, Herbert Goertz of Royalton and Thomas Roos of Dartmouth, who also spoke on ecological topics, for allowing me to absorb many of their ideas. I also thank all of the participants in the seminar for providing a stimulating atmosphere for the exchange of thought and opinions.

I would like to express my gratitude to the many friends and associates who have read all or part of the manuscript of this book and encouraged me in its production at every step of the way. Among these, some deserve special thanks for directing my attention to specific errors or for making suggestions which I eventually incorporated. In this category come Michael Greenwood, Thomas Grennes, and Katherine Dolan.

Finally, I would like to thank Susan Cook for undertaking the onerous task of typing the manuscript and helping me to distribute preliminary copies.

I would not wish to give the impression that the final responsibility for the entire work, including remaining errors and omissions, is not completely my own.

January 1971
South Royalton, Vermont

—E.G.D.

contents

TANSTAAFL*

* There ain't no such thing as a free lunch

chapter 1

WHAT ECOLOGICAL ECONOMICS IS ALL ABOUT

An Awareness of Threat

In the course of the sixties an increasing number of people in this country have begun to feel that despite the sustained growth of Gross National Product which we have experienced, something in the not too distant future looms as a threat to our unprecedentedly high standard of living. The word *ecology* is mentioned more and more frequently in connection with this sense of foreboding—could it be that ecology has taken over from economics as the "dismal science" of our day?

Ecology is the study of the interrelationships between organisms and their environment. It is distinct from the social sciences, which are concerned only with the interactions of creatures with other members of their own species, in that it stresses the ultimate mutual interdependence of all species of plant and animal life. Indeed, in its broadest sense ecology is simply a point of view which demands that we keep constantly in mind that *everything depends on everything else.*

This concept of universal mutual interdependence, at least within the extent of the market, has always been central to economics. The theory of general economic equilibrium teaches us that a change in the price or quantity produced of any good or service will affect the price and quantity produced of all other goods and services. A decline in the production of cattle will result in a decreased supply of leather. Up will go the price of leather, and hence of leather shoes. Consumers will buy fewer leather and more synthetic shoes. Workers will be laid off in the tanneries and taken on in plastics mills. Real estate values will fall in the neighborhood of the former and rise in the neighborhood of the latter. Eventually—according to economic science this is a literal certainty limited only by our ability to measure—the impact will be felt upon the price of eggs in China.

Ecological economics,[1] the subject of this book, accepts these concepts of general equilibrium and universal mutual interdependence and extends their scope to include chains of cause and effect which originate within the market, pass beyond it into the world of nature, and then return to affect human production and consumption. Sometimes the effects are direct and predictable, as when the growth of industry in the watershed of Lake Erie ruins the fishing industry there. In other cases they are dramatic and unexpected, as when the construction of the Aswan Dam in Egypt has effects which threaten to destroy more farmland than it brings into production.

The ecological effects of economic activities which pose an increasing threat to our material welfare can be classified in many fashions. One way of looking at the problem is to draw a distinction between the cumulative environmental effects of existing production and consumption activities and the additional impact arising from future economic growth and development.

Under the heading of cumulative effects we have, in the first instance, the exhaustion of irreplaceable natural resources. When the

[1] It is worth noting that etymologically the words *ecology* and *economics* are closely related. Both mean the study of, or systematization of knowledge about, the *oikos*, a Greek word meaning household.

virgin forests are cut down, the oil wells are pumped dry, and the Mesabi Range is mined out we must resort to the use of second-growth timber, oil shale, and taconite—all of which represent inferior sources which can be exploited only at increasing cost. Even these low-grade resources are not inexhaustible. Also included in the category of cumulative effects is the process of filling up irreplaceable dumping grounds with indestructible (or nearly so) waste products. For example, even if its rate of use were not to increase, the level of DDT intake of all the world's animal life would go on rising. It is already to the point where the DDT content of American mothers' milk is so high that it could not legally be bottled and sold across state lines. Likewise, the carbon dioxide content of the atmosphere, which has already risen by 14 percent in this century, would go right on rising even if our consumption of fossil fuels were to remain indefinitely at its current level.

Yet there is no prospect whatsoever that production, population, and technology will remain static. The growth of production alone means that all the cumulative effects will accumulate at an ever-increasing rate. This would be bad enough without adding the overpopulation problem. Even in the far-from-certain event that our fields, mines, and factories can supply us with the requisite quantity of artifacts, will we be able to maintain our free and individualistic life style against the sheer pressures of crowding when, by the year 2000, a world population of seven billion will have reduced elbow room per capita by more than half? Still, pollution and crowding are known horrors, and adaptable man might learn grudgingly to cope with them. It is the growth of technology which is in some ways the most frightening, since technology brings the unknown. With laboratories turning out ever more exotic drugs and chemicals at an ever-increasing rate, who will be able to test them for all their long-range and roundabout effects? How can we predict the effects of the technology of the more distant future, when we don't even know for certain what the technology of the seventies will do to us? Consider the case of the supersonic transport—scientists do not yet even know whether it will chill us by producing a layer of cirrus clouds in the stratosphere, or roast us by the greenhouse effect of the carbon dioxide it will add to the air.

Gradually, thanks to a constant stream of books, articles, speeches and TV programs, the vague ecological threat to our living standards assumes more exact contours. On one side we are faced with the prospect of simply running out of certain things which we have been consuming all along, and on the other with the prospect of devoting an ever-increasing share of our energy and ingenuity to cleaning up with our right hand the mess we make with our left.

Why are we in this quandary, and can we get out of it? The science of economics has at least some partial answers to these questions, as the next section will begin to explain.

The Spaceship Earth

Our first lesson in ecological economics will be to contrast two *models* —abstract, schematic representations—of human production and consumption. Kenneth Boulding has aptly called these the "throughput economy" and the "spaceship earth."

According to the throughput model, the economy is a device for withdrawing materials from exploitable "sources," processing and consuming them, and discarding the resultant waste products in pollutable "sinks." This process is diagrammed in Figure 1.1. The sources are the mines, wells, forests, and fields, while the sinks are rivers, oceans, holes in the ground, and wide-open spaces.

The spaceship earth model, in contrast, is based on the concept that the sources and sinks are one and the same, and that we, like the crew of a small spaceship on a long voyage, must reprocess and reuse everything that we consume. This model is represented schematically in Figure 1.2. In our spaceship earth it is our natural environment, with all of its delicate ecological interdependencies, which must serve us as both source and sink for our every act of production and consumption.

We may feel complacent about the closed-loop character of our economy as long as the process by which our wastes are returned to us is sufficiently roundabout. In times of crisis, however, the feedback path may become distressingly short. Not long ago, in a small town in Kansas, a drought dried up the river upon which the town depended for its water supply. In desperation the town simply added chlorine to its own sewage effluent and pumped it back into the water mains! [2]

The significance of these two models for ecological economics lies in the fact that although the spaceship earth is the more accurate representation of reality, our economic system is adapted to cope only with the throughput model.

The first great defect of our throughput-oriented economic

[2] This example is reported by Robert and Leona Rienow, *Moment in the Sun*, p. 132.

FIGURE 1.1 The throughput economy

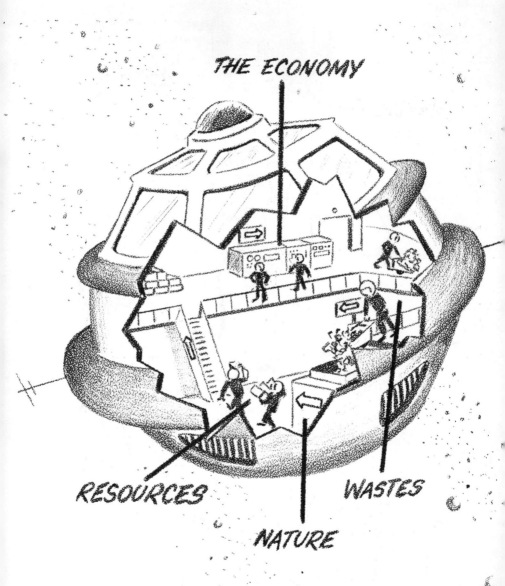

FIGURE 1.2 The spaceship earth

system is the way in which it distributes costs and benefits. As we have already pointed out, every action which we undertake as a producer or a consumer sets off a chain reaction which in some way affects the opportunities for production and consumption available to every other individual on the globe. In a market economy money and prices are used to keep account of the costs and benefits which this process brings to every individual. For example, you will purchase this book only if the benefit to you of reading it, as measured by the amount of money or other goods you are willing to exchange to obtain it, is sufficient to compensate the publishing house, the typesetter, the editor, the salesman, the papermaker, the inkmaker, and the author for the costs and troubles we incurred in the process of producing it. Yet, as a consumer you need to know nothing at all about the process of bookmaking to know exactly how much all of these costs will add up to, since the market price of the book summarizes them in an easily understood form.

This is what is meant when we say that the price system in a market economy is a system of *social accounting* which keeps track of the costs and benefits all along the chain of cause and effect set off by the production or consumption of any good.

How thorough is this accounting system? We have already seen that it keeps track of the direct costs of producing the book, but there are other types of costs which the price system in our throughput economy does a poor job of keeping account of. These are costs which result when one of those chains of cause and effect passes out of the realm of the market into the natural environment, and then sneaks back in to upset production and consumption patterns elsewhere. Does the price you pay for this book reflect the cost borne by those who live downstream from the paper mill where this page was rolled off and who have their fishing and swimming ruined? No it does not. Does the price reflect the loss to the birdwatcher who used to seek his quarry in the woodlands that were cut down to make the pulp for the paper? No. How about the neighbor to the printing plant whose sleep is disturbed by the traffic noise every night when the shift changes? Unfortunately, the price system does not keep track of this cost either.

In addition to the inability of the price system to keep accurate account of costs and benefits, our throughput economy has another serious fault. This lies in the way in which the overall results of economic activity are measured. The most popular measure of economic performance, one which we can follow closely in the newspaper, is Gross National Product. This is a figure, in the neighborhood of one trillion dollars for the United States as this book goes to press, which purports to measure the sum total value of all the goods and services produced for production and investment in the country during a year.

We are consistently taught to take pride in the GNP as a measure of our well being. We doff our hats to the Japanese, whose GNP grows at a rate in excess of 10 percent per year. We shed a tear for the Nepalese, whose GNP of $50 or so per capita is the lowest in the world. And in the CIA, specialists pore over the latest data on the GNP of the Soviet Union like bookies over their racing forms. Does all this GNP fetishism make sense? Let us examine a somewhat fanciful example to see why it may not.

Suppose we have a peaceful little country with a per capita GNP of $100, all produced by the women, who work the fields in the morning and gossip in the afternoon, while the men do nothing at all but sit around and play cards and drink tea all day. Suppose now that an enterprising foreign businessman sets up a soap factory and puts all of the men to work, each producing an average of $40 worth of soap a year. Previously there was no market for soap in this pastoral nation, but now, as the soap factory is belching black coal smoke from its boilers which soil everybody's curtains, the entire output of the factory is sold to local housewives, who now spend all of their afternoons at the laundromat.

Question: What has happened to the GNP of this country? As any graduate of Economics 1 will tell you, it has gone up by 20 percent, to $120 per capita. Agricultural output has not fallen, and industrial production of $20 per capita has been introduced. *Question:* What has happened to the level of well being of the inhabitants of this country? They have no more to eat than before; their curtains are no cleaner than before; and they are working four times as long. Ergo, they are, let us say, about one-quarter as well off as before.

There is a serious lesson to be learned from this little fable; namely, that GNP is not a measure of well being but simply a measure of throughput. It measures the rate at which the crank is turning on that meat grinder in Figure 1.1. A person's welfare does not depend on this rate of flow of material and energy through the system, but on a *state of affairs* which the throughput process serves to maintain and improve. Just stop to think about it. We are happy when we can bring about a condition in which we are warm, well-clothed, stomach full, and in good company. The irksome thing about life is that just as we get this set up, it starts to go to pieces. Our house cools down; our clothes wear out; the food in our stomachs is digested and eliminated; and our friends go home when the bottle runs dry. That is where GNP comes in—it is our weapon against entropy and decay. We generate GNP in order to fuel the furnace, wash our clothes, and so forth.

Are we better off when we have more GNP? Not necessarily. Think what happens to GNP, for example, as the seasons change. In January it takes a massive rate of throughput to keep your furnace fired—lots of GNP. In the summer your air conditioner sucks up huge quantities of GNP to keep you cool. But on that rare day in spring, when you throw open all the windows and *feel* like a million dollars, GNP takes a nose dive!

It would be an exaggeration to pretend that GNP and welfare are completely unrelated. When you average out things like seasonal and climatic differences there is a rough correspondence between the comfort and complexity of the state of life one trys to maintain and the amount of throughput necessary to maintain it. Clearly the fact that our per capita GNP is some thirty times that of Nepal has something to do with the fact that we are surrounded with some high multiple of the quantity of creature comforts of the Nepalese—and must keep all in working order.

Why should we quibble about GNP, which is, after all, only a number? Shouldn't we be concerned about real problems and policies instead? Unfortunately, it is impossible to separate the two, for policies are often made not on the basis of reality but on the basis of appearance. The ways in which the results of a policy are measured may crucially affect its formulation. The means our government takes to fight inflation and unemployment, erase the balance of payments deficit, or try to show a surplus in the federal budget are all crucially affected by the arbitrary choices which economists and statisticians must make among alternative ways of measuring these things.

The same is true of GNP. As long as we base our national economic goals on a number which measures throughput rather than welfare, you can be sure that the government will do everything in its power to maximize the growth of throughput regardless of the effect on welfare.

What we need is a neat, eye-catching summary statistic which will protect us from the fallacy that throughput maximization is a good thing. One simple idea, which is beginning to catch on, is simply to rename this same number and call it Gross National Cost. Another idea is to ask our statisticians to deduct from the magic number the cash value of all the damage done during the year by the spillages, leakages, seepages, emission, effluents, and cacaphony that spill out of our meat-grinder economy along with the meat. Still another idea is, I think, the best of all. This is to split the current single GNP figure into two components. The first—call it Type I GNP—would measure that fraction of GNP which was produced with *renewable* resources and *recyclable* wastes. Type II GNP would then measure the total value of production which was based on the exhaustion of irreplaceable resources and the production of indestructible wastes.[3]

If this distinction were made, it would be clear that the production of clean, Type I GNP was an indisputable boon to mankind, while the output of dirty Type II GNP was at best a temporary welfare gain at the expense of further destruction of our environment. Politicians and economists would then design their policies to maximize Type I and minimize Type II. In the eyes of world opinion a high Type I component would be a source of national pride, while high production of the Type II variety would be a source of shame.

The power of statistics to determine policy should never be underestimated. If ecological economists could win the battle of the National Income Accounts their overall job would be three-quarters complete.

Ideology, Ecology, and the TANSTAAFL Principle

Faced with a steadily deteriorating environment and a set of social and economic institutions which are incapable of even correctly measuring this deterioration, let alone reversing it, an increasing number of voices are being raised with explanations of the causes of the crisis and with proposals for ending it. Although the analyses and solutions are almost as numerous and varied as the individuals propounding them, there are at least two general groupings or schools of thought—what might almost be called two ecological ideologies.

[3] The idea of separating Type I and Type II GNP was suggested to me by Herbert Goertz. In a sense, it is an extreme extension of the concept of *Net* National Product, a figure derived from *Gross* National Product by deducting the sum total of depreciation of capital equipment. To arrive at Type I GNP one must also deduct the "depreciation" of all natural sources and sinks.

The first ideology can be called ecological evangelism. At the root of the environmental crisis the ecological evangelists see the sins of ignorance, indifference, and greed. The tone and the content of their writing is tailored accordingly.

Their tone is one of moral outrage. Very typical are the comments of Robert and Leona Rienow in the introduction to their book, *Moment in the Sun.* The authors explain how they began with thirty feet of files on the subject of the environment and the intention of writing an analytical, dispassionate study of what is happening in America today. However, four years, twenty-five thousand miles of traveling, and countless interviews later they wrote:

> We surrendered the impossible job of impersonal analysis of a deeply personal matter. We gave up computer thinking on a subject that cannot be computerized, a subject which means your future and ours, the future of the land and the whole American people. We are involved. We are biased for beauty. We are the unblushing partisans of restraint in both exploitation and breeding. We are pluggers for a new, hard look at our misdeeds, for painful self-sacrifice, if need be, to "hold this land" and what is still on it.[4]

The content of the writing of the ecological evangelists reflects their analysis of individual moral failure as the source of the problem. They preach, first of all, of the need for ecological education and ecological enlightenment. Their first principle is that ignorance is no excuse, that it is immoral to take any action, to produce or consume any product without knowing what effects that act of production or consumption will have on the environment. If only people *realized* that in purchasing redwood lawn chairs and leopard skin coats they were threatening these species of plant and animal life with extinction, perhaps they would think twice before buying. And if manufacturers of new drugs, chemicals, and pesticides would simply bother to *investigate* the effects of their products on life cycles and food chains, instead of just marketing anything not definitely known to be harmful, perhaps much destruction could be avoided.

Next after enlightenment the evangelists preach the virtue of environmental sensitivity. They realize that ignorance is not always the problem and that, in fact, some people exist who are so insensitive to

[4] Rienow and Rienow, p. vii.

the beauty of nature that they would knowingly prefer their cheap lawn furniture to a noble stand of redwoods; would prefer a leopard lined with silk and flaunted on Fifth Avenue in New York City to one creeping through the jungles blending with light and shadow; that they would prefer the convenience of cheap newsprint to the beauty of clear running streams and rivers; and would prefer the thrill of gunning their 400 horsepower coffin from stoplight to stoplight to having the tonic of clean air to breathe. Nonetheless, although the insensitive may be more of a problem than the ignorant, they are not beyond salvation. There is always the hope that if the beauty of nature and the banality of commercial civilization can be put into words, pictures, or testimonials sufficiently eloquent and vivid, the insensitive may be made aware of the lack of sophistication of their current tastes and be converted to the cult of nature.

After having disposed of the ignorant and indifferent, the ecological evangelists turn their energies to the last and most recalcitrant group, those avaricious and malevolent souls who would willingly and knowingly rape the wilderness to turn a profit for themselves. These, if they cannot be brought to their senses by the preaching of the Christian virtue of altruism, must then be subjected to pressure, protest, legislation, or even guerrilla action to force them into adopting a more public-spirited attitude.

At this point the ideology of ecological evangelism begins to shade over into what can be called ecological radicalism. Ecological radicals are less prone to blame the crisis on the sins of individuals and more likely to blame "the system." Very typical of ecological radicalism are the views of the editors of *Ramparts,* who recently wrote:

> . . . as long as society organizes production around the incentive to convert man's energies and nature's resources into profit, no planned, equable (sic), ecologically balanced system of production can ever exist. . . .
>
> We must, in short, junk the business system and its way of life, and create revolutionary new institutions to embody new goals—human and environmental.
>
> All this sounds utopian. Well, utopias are relative. More utopian by far than revolution is the idea that the present society, dominated by business, can create lasting, meaningful reforms sufficient, for example, to permit mankind to survive this century.[5]

[5] *Ramparts,* May 1970, p. 4.

The cumulative effect of the voices of the ecological evangelists, of ecological radicals, and of ordinary concerned citizens to whom no ideological label applies is to produce increasingly irresistible demands for massive governmental action to do something now to stop the deterioration of the environment. Washington responds as best it knows how, with a plethora of proposals to ban this or that product, regulate this or that industry, require this or that device, or purchase this or that tract of land for a national park.

Speaking now as an economist, as an economist with a definite concern for piloting our spaceship earth safely through the ecological crisis with which we are increasingly undeniably faced, I must say that listening to all of this ecological dialogue sets off a great number of red flashing warning lights on my control panel. These warn that in the name of ecological salvation we are in danger of being led by men of the greatest good will and the best intentions down the road to some grave social and economic mistakes, which have been made too many times before in too many countries to bear repeating here and now again. I will mention just three of these dangers before going on, in succeeding chapters, to suggest some means for avoiding them.

The first warning light flashes when I hear the call for self-sacrifice and self-restraint as the means for resolving the environmental crisis. Any economist worth his salt knows that altruism is notoriously weak as a force for social change, and that the goal of avoiding ecological disaster will be more easily and rapidly reached by methods which harness the strong human motivations—the greed, avarice, and self-interest of individuals within the ranks of business, government, and consumers. We simply do not have time to wait for an ethical revolution before we clean up.

The second warning light flashes when I hear impassioned and contemptuous denunciations of the tastes and values of affluent American consumers. Again, impatience is part of the reason for these misgivings. Knowing how slow to change are the underlying preference systems of the individuals who inhabit our society, the economist tends to seek more speedy solutions to social problems which work within current tastes and preferences. An equal cause for concern is that certain special interest elites among environmental activists will take advantage of the genuine common interest in environmental reform, shared by all the people, to shape public policy to suit their own allegedly superior tastes and preferences.

The third warning light on my panel goes off when I hear demands that the business system, the profit motive, and private property be scrapped in favor of a "planned, equitable, and ecologically balanced system of production." Application of elementary principles of economics suggests that the path to a planned, equitable, and ecologically balanced system of production is more likely to be through a strengthening of the business system, private property, and the profit motive than through their abolition. Even if there were no other evidence, a look at the wholesale rape of the environment which has been conducted in the name of building socialism in the planned economy of the Soviet Union should be sufficient proof.[6]

But the purpose of this book is not simply to criticize the well-intentioned suggestions of others. More importantly, it is to expound a constructive strategy of its own for coping with the environmental crisis.

The fundamental principle on which this strategy is built may be expressed in a simple slogan—There Ain't No Such Thing As A Free Lunch—the "TANSTAAFL principle," for short.[7] The TANSTAAFL principle is closely related to the fundamental theorem of ecological economics, that everything depends on everything else. Everything worth while has a cost. Whenever you think you are getting something for nothing, look again—someone, somewhere, somehow is paying for it. Behind every free lunch there is a hidden cost to be accounted for.

The task of ecological economics is to figure out how to restructure the economic system so that these hidden costs will be brought out into the open, with the ultimate aim that no one who benefits from the use of the environment will be able to escape without paying in full. The rest of this book is devoted to working out specific applications of this general strategy in order to deal with specific problems.

First, Chapter 2 will review some of the basic principles of economics which lead to the conclusions suggested in this introduction. Without some basic tools of analysis there is no hope for raising the

[6] See Marshall Goldman, "The Convergence of Environmental Disruption," *Science*, October 2, 1970.
[7] The fundamental importance of this principle, and the expression itself, were impressed upon me by Robert Heinlein's fascinating ecological novel, *The Moon Is a Harsh Mistress* (New York: George Putnam's Sons, 1966). Students of the natural sciences will recognize the close relationship between the TANSTAAFL principle and the Second Law of Thermodynamics.

discussion of economics and ecology above the level of unsubstantiated polemic. With these tools in hand we' will then examine in more detail the weaknesses of our social and economic system which have led us to the point of crisis.

Chapter 3 will demonstrate that it is possible to construct a condemnation of the polluters and abusers of our environment on a sound rational basis, without resort to the weaker support of romantic emotionalism or offended special interest. It will be shown that stopping the destruction of the environment, properly considered, is not the special interest of any group but is in an important sense in the general interest of all, polluters and victims alike. Some guidelines will be offered for public policy in the area of pollution control.

Chapter 4 will add the caveat that despite the demonstrable existence of a common interest in environmental improvement, there are many pitfalls in the path of any attempt to organize politically for the realization of this common interest. In addition, some further theoretical tools will be introduced as a basis for the discussion of three special problems. These are the problem of population control, in Chapter 5, the problem of economic development and the international allocation of resources, in Chapter 6, and the problem of preserving the wilderness, in Chapter 7.

The concluding chapter will turn attention from these microeconomic problems to discuss some important issues of ecological macroeconomics, such as, can man survive?

chapter 2

PRINCIPLES OF ECONOMICS IN ONE EASY LESSON

Picture two men who are having a race. Each is given certain equipment at the starting line: 1. a pair of tennis shoes and 2. a box of bicycle parts. When the starting gun goes off each man can proceed in either of two ways. He can put on the tennis shoes and start running toward the finish line or, alternatively, he can sit down, assemble the bicycle, and then ride it to the finish. Which is the best way to win the race? Clearly, the answer depends on the length of the racecourse. If it were one hundred yards, there is no doubt that it would be faster to run. But if it were twenty-five miles or more, the bicycle method would probably be the best bet—the rider would breeze past the exhausted runner at about the fifteen-mile mark and coast on to an easy victory.

Economists deal with situations like this every day. The time you put in on the starting line getting your equipment ready is called *investment*—a term denoting activity that does not in itself get you any closer to your goal but which allows you to proceed faster later on. The optimal amount of investment depends, among other things, on how big a job you have to do.

Getting through this little book on ecological economics is a medium-sized job, so before proceeding, we will digress to make a medium-sized investment in some special concepts and terminology. Any reader who thinks he can run faster than he can ride can skip ahead to the next chapter, but it isn't advisable.

Marginalism and the Law of Supply and Demand

The first useful economic concept needed in succeeding chapters is that of *marginalism*. Economists are always talking about marginal this and marginal that because most of the important economic decisions made in this world are marginal decisions—whether to do a little bit more of this or a little bit more of something else—rather than large, all-or-nothing decisions. For example, we notice that although an occasional consumer may come to a spiritual crisis in his life and, as a matter of religious principle, decide to foreswear meat and become a vegetarian, most consumers do not make all-or-nothing decisions concerning meat and vegetables. Instead, they make marginal decisions such as whether to buy ten carrots and five slices of salami, or to cut back by one carrot in order to get one more slice of salami. In business, marginal decisions are also the focus of everyday attention. Although occasionally momentous, all-or-nothing decisions may be made, such as whether or not to build a transcontinental railroad (there is, by definition, no such thing as half a transcontinental railroad) most railroad managers spend most of their time making thousands of small decisions—whether to add one more car to the 2:52 train from Chicago to Minneapolis. Even economic changes which in retrospect appear to be radical and sweeping (the Industrial Revolution, the mechanization of agriculture) usually turn out, upon close inspection, to have been composed of a great many small, marginal decisions.

Economists who have analyzed the behavior of individuals and households in their role as consumers have found that consumer decisions made according to the marginal principle best serve the goal of gaining maximum benefit from a limited budget. In deciding whether or not to make a marginal increase in his consumption of one item the consumer must judge whether the *marginal benefit* of extending consumption in this direction is sufficient to compensate for the loss of the opportunity to extend his consumption in some other direction. For example, at the lunch counter if I spend a dime on one more cup of coffee, I must forego the opportunity to spend that dime on one more donut; hence, before I make the decision I subconsciously ask myself whether the marginal benefit I would receive from a dime's worth of coffee is greater than that from a dime's worth of donut.

It seems to be an almost universal law of consumer behavior that as a person consumes more and more of a given good, the marginal benefit to him of still more of it becomes less and less. That first piece of chocolate cake may be delightful; the second is merely good; the third is about all that the consumer can hold; and the fourth may send him off to the vomitorium. This is the *law of diminishing marginal benefit.*

The law of diminishing marginal benefit is what guarantees that the normal consumer will purchase a wide variety of goods, for if he bought too much of a single item its marginal benefit would fall below that of the foregone opportunities, and he would not be getting the most benefit for his money. This is just common sense. The only time the law of diminishing marginal benefit seems to be violated is in the phenomenon of addiction. The addict, craving more of the object of his habit the more he consumes, may spend every cent he has on this one thing.

In the business world the marginal concept is also central to the decision-making process, but this time it is *marginal cost* which is the focus of attention. The typical avaricious Capitalist, always looking for a way to increase his profits, will produce anything which he thinks he can sell above the cost. Suppose, for example, he owns a farm and is trying to decide whether or not to plant a few more turnips. If an additional pound of turnips can be sold for ten cents, he will simply compare this to the marginal cost of growing a pound of turnips. If the marginal cost of turnips is, say, five cents a pound, he will be able to pocket a five-cent profit after paying his costs out of the increased sales revenue.

What keeps greedy Capitalists from turning the whole world into one giant turnip patch? Two things. First of all, there is the law of diminishing returns, which says that if you devote more and more resources to any given line of production, eventually the marginal cost of production will rise. In the case of turnips, eventually you will run out of good turnip fields and have to grow your turnips in poorer fields where each additional pound of turnips will cost you eight, ten, even twenty cents. And when the marginal cost goes above the price any smart Capitalist will get out of the turnip business, since the opportunity for profit will be gone.

Second, the law of diminishing marginal benefit puts another brake on the expansion of turnip production. Although consumers may at first eagerly snap them up at ten cents, as the market is flooded with an ever-greater supply of turnips, the benefit of an additional turnip, and hence the price which a customer will pay for it, will gradually fall. The falling marginal benefit will at some point meet the rising marginal cost and a price will be established, perhaps eight cents a pound, where there will be no further incentive to expand production.

Taken together, the law of diminishing marginal benefit and the law of diminishing returns (that is, increasing marginal costs) form the basis for the famous *law of supply and demand.* The amount of a good *demanded* by consumers depends on its price because, desiring to get the most for their money, they will purchase it only as long as its marginal benefit exceeds its price. With diminishing marginal benefits, this means a fall in the price will induce consumers to buy more, and a rise in the price to buy less. The amount of a product *supplied* by producers also depends on price—but because of increasing marginal costs, suppliers will step up their output only if the price rises, and will cut back when it falls. If, at a given price, the desired purchases of consumers exceed the desired sales of producers, the pressure of unsatisfied customers competing to buy a limited supply will bid up the price, and will, consequently, call for a greater supply of the good. If the price is such that desired sales exceed desired purchases, the opposite happens; unsatisfied sellers, competing for a limited number of customers, drive the price down, inducing the customers to buy more.

Somewhere between these two possibilities is a point where the desired sales of suppliers and desired purchases of consumers just match. The forces of the market always tend to drive the price toward this point, which is the point where marginal benefit = price = marginal cost.

Efficiency and the Equimarginal Principle

Marginalism is just one of the peculiar concepts that economists always seem to be hung up about. Another of equal importance is the concept of *efficiency*. The common dictionary definition of efficiency is the quality or property of acting or producing with a minimum of waste, expense, or unnecessary effort. That's actually not a bad definition, and if we were to limit ourselves to it, we could probably get along fairly well. Still, as long as this is a book on economics we may as well use the more pedantic sounding but more interesting technical definition favored by economists. An economy is said to be efficient at a given moment in time if and only if there is no way in which goods and services can be redistributed among consumers, or production tasks reassigned among producers, in such a way that as a result the welfare of at least one individual is increased without a decrease in the welfare of any other individual.

The economic definition of efficiency allows us to deal with certain situations where the ordinary definition would seem awkward. For example, what about the possibility mentioned above that the entire world might be turned into a gigantic turnip plantation? Suppose that all the men, land, and machines in the world were put to work producing turnips, all using the most modern techniques and working with an absolute minimum of waste, expense, or unnecessary effort. Would this be an efficient use of the world's resources? According to the dictionary definition, yes. According to the economic definition, no.

The turnip plantation model of the world economy would not be efficient because it ignores the law of diminishing marginal benefits, and its corollary that in diversity is bliss. (We will not consider the possibilty that all the world's consumers are turnip *addicts*.) A man hour diverted from turnip production would decrease the turnip output by a small amount, but because of the huge turnip surplus and the incredible shortage of all other foods that man hour could produce a much greater benefit if devoted, let us say, to potatoes. The worker could be paid just as much for growing potatoes as turnips, and some lucky consumer would get the enormous benefit of variety in his diet. No one would be worse off, and at least one person would be better off; hence, the original situation, by our definition, could not have been efficient. Only when the world's resources were employed with a minimum of waste, expense, and unnecessary effort, *and* were employed producing the proper variety and diversity of goods and services in accordance with the law of diminishing marginal benefit would economic efficiency be attained.

But how do we know what is just the "proper" variety and diversity of goods and services? To answer this question we must apply what economists call the *equimarginal* principle. This principle has several aspects, some of which have been hinted at already. We saw before that I would be spending my lunch budget efficiently if I divided my money between coffee and donuts in such a way that the *marginal benefit* of a dime's worth of donuts would be *equal* to the *marginal benefit* of a dime's worth of coffee. If this principle were applied for each consumer and for all goods worldwide, one requirement for worldwide efficiency of resource allocation would be satisfied.

Another aspect of the equimarginal principle which must hold for efficient use of resources is that the *marginal benefit* to the consumer must *equal* the *marginal cost* to the producer for each item produced. The truth of this statement can be illustrated with a counterexample. If the lunch counter of the previous example can produce coffee at a marginal cost of four cents per cup, and I have to pay ten cents for it, an opportunity for mutual gain is being passed up. I will stop consumption, as we have already seen, when the marginal benefit to me of coffee falls to ten cents a cup, although I might be willing to pay as much as seven cents for still another. It is clear that if I made a special deal with the waitress and got a refill for five cents, I would get seven cents worth of benefit, the counter would get one cent worth of profit, and efficiency would be improved.

As an exercise the reader may wish to work out still another application of the equimarginal principle: Efficiency requires, when a given product is produced by two or more producers, that the marginal cost of production be the same for every producer.

The Invisible Hand

Making sure that the equimarginal principle is applied and that production and consumption are carried out efficiently on a worldwide scale is no mean trick. There are nearly four billion people in the world, most of them functioning in a dual role as producers and consumers, and heaven only knows how many hundreds of thousands or millions of separate and distinct goods and services are being produced. Applying the equimarginal principle on a worldwide scale, or even on a nationwide or citywide scale, necessarily requires an enormous network of communications and system of incentives. Communications are necessary, for how is one producer going to set his marginal cost equal to that of all others, or how is a consumer to buy eggs up to the point where marginal benefit declines to meet the marginal cost, or how are any of a number of other similar equimarginal conditions to be met, if all these quantities are not universally known? Yet communications alone is not enough, for what is to keep a producer from allowing his marginal cost to drift above or below the mark, or consumers to slip up with their marginal benefits, and so on, if each of these individuals does not have some incentive to pay attention to the proper quantities when they are communicated to him?

Various systems for maintaining communications and incentives could be imagined, and many have been tried—for example, providing communications by printing all the marginal costs and benefits in the newspaper every day, in tiny type like the stock market reports; and providing incentives by sending around a member of the King's Own Guard to beat up anyone who chose to ignore them. Or we could try having everyone send data on punchcards to the Central Statistical Agency, and solve the whole resource allocation problem on a giant computer, mailing a notice to each citizen with weekly production and consumption plans, and rewarding those who met the plans by placing a gold star beside their name on a chart at City Hall. Schemes like these have long been favored by all manner of utopians and social reformers and, with minor variations, many economies or at least parts of many economies in the world today are run according to principles of this general nature.

Other economies or parts of economies use a different type of communications and incentive mechanism known as the *competitive market*. In such an economy the chief means of communication is the price system. Since, as we saw above, the law of supply and demand in a competitive market tends to fix the price of a product at a level where marginal cost = price = marginal benefit, a knowledge of the prices of each product produced is all that a producer or consumer needs in order to apply the equimarginal principle if he so wishes. The incentive to do so comes, for the greedy Capitalistic producer, in the form of the profit motive—obeying the rule marginal cost = price will not only guarantee economic efficiency, about which the producer presumably cares not at all, but will also guarantee a maximum profit, for which he is presumably willing to slave day and night. For the consumer, equally indifferent to and even more likely ignorant of the principles of efficient resource allocation, the incentive to obey the equimarginal principle comes from the spur of necessity—unless his pay-check is bigger than mine, he will be very prudent in spending it to get the maximum possible benefit out of his limited budget, which he can do only by consciously or unconsciously equating the marginal benefits of the last penny's worth of each different good he consumes.

The eighteenth-century British economist Adam Smith was among the first to realize the efficiency with which the price system solved the problems of communication and incentives, of coordinating the selfish activities of producers and consumers to promote the socially desirable goal of rational resource allocation. Competition within the framework of the market economy seemed to him to be an "invisible hand" which, operating through the self-interest of the butcher and the baker and entirely without central calculation or control, supplied the populace with their daily bread and meat.

Cough, gasp! says the skeptical reader. If this invisible hand is so great, why can't it guide some self-interested soul to supply me with breathable air along with my meat and bread? And do I have to put up with that stinking cesspool of a river outside my window just because some invisible hand says I do? What about that SST that just flew overhead, did the invisible hand put that there, too? Or does the invisible hand need a big invisible handcuff if we are going to survive ecological disaster?

These are valid and challenging questions which the science of ecological economics must face. In reality, markets are not always per-fect and don't always work. The price system does not always function smoothly, nor does it always lead to application of the equimarginal principle. A society is not necessarily desirable from every point of view just because it is efficient (although it is necessarily undesirable from any point of view if it is inefficient, taking the full definition of efficiency into account). It is so easy to find valid fault with the operation of the price system as it exists in the United States today that it is tempting to eliminate market mechanisms from consideration altogether as a means of coping with the environmental crisis.

In the following chapters, however, I will attempt time and again to make the point that the simple economic principles expounded by Adam Smith, elaborated by economists over the course of two hundred years, and presented here "in one easy lesson" can be ignored by would-be ecological reformers only at their peril. There is a lot of life left in the old invisible hand yet if we will just take the time to figure out how to put it to work.

chapter 3

POLLUTION AND THE PRICE SYSTEM

The Invisible Hand Slips Up

The first thing which comes to mind for most people, when they think of the environmental crisis, is pollution. The population explosion, the disappearance of the wilderness, the exhaustion of the world's supply of oil and copper ore, imminent though some say they are, seem remote by comparsion. Today *The New York Times* can print a map showing an ominous black splotch, representing the danger area with more than .10 parts per million of sulphur dioxide in the air spreading over most of Manhattan. The death of Lake Erie and the famous Cuyahoga River fire are almost matters of ancient history. Even in pastoral Vermont, the number of different shots needed before diving in at the local swimming hole serves as a reminder that no place is safe. As far away as the Antarctic, the penguins are said to have DDT in their blood. Is all this the *unavoidable* price of progress with which we must simply learn to live? The answer to this question is partly yes, but mostly no.

It is partly yes, because of the TANSTAAFL principle. Everything good has a price, and that includes a price for clean air, clean water, virgin forests, and quiet streets. We can have a little more of this only at the expense of a little less of that, and only the addict will choose to expend all of his resources on one item without regard for the alternatives foregone. Surely most of us would permit a few trees to be cut down to prevent the monotony of row upon row of cinderblock houses and room upon room of plastic furniture. We would consider tolerating the exhaust of a few cars and planes rather than live the stultifying life of a man who never travels beyond the confines of the county where he was born. A world totally without pollution, a world in which all of nature was labeled "look, don't touch" would be too poor in other things to be the object of our aspirations.

But although for most of us the best of all possible worlds would contain some nonzero degree of pollution, it does not necessarily mean that our market economy gives us *just the right* amount. It does not do so, and would not, in fact, even if it were a perfectly functioning market free of all the problems of monopolies, immobilities, ignorance, dysfunctional traditions and prejudices, and so on which beset the real world. From the point of view of ecological economics the basic flaw in the theory of the efficient, self-regulating market economy is that the price system, as it currently exists, is suitable for use *only in the throughput economy*. As soon as we develop an awareness that we are living not in a throughput economy but aboard the spaceship earth, we can begin to see that Adam Smith's invisible hand is no longer so reliable as we once thought.

To see why this is so, let us look at a simple example. Figure 3.1 is a map showing the location of industry along the banks of a certain river. Along the higher reaches several paper mills are located. These produce, along with paper, quite a bit of waste material, which is dumped directly into the river. Somewhat farther downstream there is a water works, which draws water from the river and purifies it to serve the needs of a small town located nearby.

An investigation of the economics of paper production and water purification reveals the following situation: The paper mills, taken

PAPER MILLS

WATER WORKS

FIGURE 3.1 Map

together, are producing 10 tons of paper per day. The mill owners have found that an additional dollar spent on the production of paper (properly allocated to the purchase of additional labor, machinery, and raw materials) will give an increase in output of 200 pounds. Our investigation further reveals that these paper mills are competitive profit maximizers, as good Capitalist firms should be, and are thus selling their product at a price of 1/2 cent per pound, just equal to marginal cost. Down at the water works, the cost situation is slightly more complicated. The chief engineer knows that the basic cost of pumping water from the river and filtering out the natural sediments is a constant 50 cents per 1,000 gallons. However, the effluent from the paper mills complicates the water purification process. In fact, for each ton of paper produced, it is necessary to spend an extra five cents per 1,000 gallons on additional filtration and chemical treatment of the river water before it becomes fit to drink. At the moment, then, with paper output at ten tons per day, the cost of water is one dollar per thousand gallons. The water works is not a competitive firm, but a wise economist on the city council has decreed that water should be sold at marginal cost anyhow. At the price of a dollar per 1,000 gallons, 100,000 gallons of water are sold each day in the community.

The consumers in this town, like consumers everywhere, are interested in spending their limited budgets on paper and water in such a way as to get a maximum of satisfaction. Finding water available at 1/10 of a cent per gallon and paper at 1/2 cent per pound, they adjust their consumption of the two products until the satisfaction they would get from an additional pound of paper is just equal to that which would be yielded by 5 more gallons of water.

From our previous discussion we might be tempted to conclude that the situation just described would be a classic example of efficient allocation of resources via the market. When producers sell their product at marginal cost, and consumers adjust their consumption to equate the marginal benefit of a penny's worth of each product, the equimarginal principle is satisfied—or has something been left out? Let us check to see whether our previous reasoning remains valid when dealing with an economic situation in which the throughput assumption is violated, as it is in this case by the existence of the environmental feedback link of the river which serves simultaneously as a pollutable *sink* for the paper mill and as an exploitable *source* for the water works.

In order for resources to be allocated efficiently, as we saw above, consumers must pursue each line of consumption exactly to the point where the marginal benefit of an additional unit expenditure exactly balances the marginal benefit of the opportunities foregone. Where only the two goods, water and paper, exist this rule means that paper must be consumed to the point where the benefit yielded by an additional penny's worth (2 pounds) of paper just equals the benefit which would be yielded by the quantity of water which must be sacrificed in order to obtain that 2 pounds of paper.

This is just where the catch comes in. In the market the consumers, ignorant of the technology of paper and water production, must depend on the price system to tell them how much water must be foregone to get 2 pounds of paper. The answer given by the price system is 5 gallons. Despite the fact that the prices of both paper and water are equal to their marginal costs, this is the *wrong* answer.

To answer the question of how much water must be given up to gain a pound of paper correctly, let us perform a simple experiment. Shift $1.00 worth of productive resources out of the production of water and put them to work in one of the paper mills. Since the marginal cost of water is 1/10 cent per gallon, we know that diverting the dollar's worth of resources from the water works will cause a drop in output of 1000 gallons, leaving a total output of 99,000 gallons per day. Since the marginal cost of paper is 1/2 cent per pound, this same unit of resources will be capable of adding 200 pounds per day to the output of the paper mill, where it is put to work. The immediate result of the resource shift is to exchange 1,000 gallons of water for 200 pounds of paper, a 5:1 ratio just equal to the ratio of marginal costs, the price ratio, and the consumers' marginal benefit ratio.

However, we cannot leave things at that. So far we have not taken into account the effect of the environmental link between paper and water production. A few hours or a few days after this initial resource shift has been made, the effect will begin to be noticed down at the water works, for the 200 pound step up in paper production will result in a proportionate increase in effluent discharge upstream. Since each ton of paper production adds 5 cents to the cost of water purification, we know that the cost of water purification will go up exactly from $1.00 to $1.005, or by 0.5 percent. This additional cost means that the $99 worth of resources left at the water works can no longer process the same amount of water as before. In fact, output at the water works will drop by approximately an additional 500 gallons to 98,500 gallons. Our conclusion must be that the extra 200 pounds of paper which were gained by the transfer of a dollar's worth of resources required the sacrifice not of 1,000 gallons but of 1,500 gallons of water, half again as much as we would have predicted from looking at the price ratio!

This means that the economy is not giving the consumers in town the greatest possible satisfaction from the productive resources which they are paying to have employed in the two lines of production. Consumers misled by market prices into thinking they must forego only 5 gallons of water to gain a pound of paper, demand relatively too much paper. If they knew that the benefit foregone was that of 7-1/2 gallons of water, they would switch their consumption patterns in favor of water. Workers would be laid off in the paper mills and taken on in the water works until the falling marginal benefit of water and the rising marginal benefit of paper were brought into the 7-1/2 to 1 ratio. Then, and only then, would the equimarginal principle be satisfied.

If an economy is inefficient, as this one was before we came upon the scene, it will always be possible to draw up some sort of a contract of agreement which would be voluntarily acceptable by all participants in the economy, that is, which would benefit at least one of them without making any of them worse off. In the case under discussion the possibility for such an agreement does exist.[1] For example, we might propose a multilateral contract which would be signed 1. by all consumers in the community (say there are 200 of them) who would each agree to buy 1 pound less of paper and in return receive a special coupon entitling them to buy 6 gallons of water for the price which they would normally have to pay for 5; 2. by the 5 paper mill owners, who would each agree to release 20 cents worth of resources from the production of paper and in return get 10 free gallons of water; and 3. by the director of the water works, who would agree to spend $1.00 more on the purification of water provided that the other parties kept their parts of the bargain. It is clear that each group would profit from this. The consumers, who had previously adjusted their paper and water purchases to the point where they placed equal value on 1 pound of paper and 5 gallons of water would be getting a bonus of 1 gallon above and beyond the bare minimum 5 gallons, which they would accept in exchange for giving up 1 pound of paper. The paper producer

[1] The reader should be cautioned that the significance of the agreement proposed here is primarily theoretical rather than practical. See Chapter 4 below.

would lose 40 pounds of paper production, and hence 20 cents in revenue, by cutting back his productive expenditures 20 cents, but would be compensated by the bonus of 10 gallons of free water, which he could use himself or sell at the market price. The director of the water works would incur an increase in costs of $1.00 but because of the reduction in pollution would gain from the deal not 1,000 but 1,500 gallons of added production. He would make back his added costs on the 1,200 gallons which he sold to consumers at the reduced price of 1/12 cent per gallon, would give away 50 gallons free to the mill owners in that part of the bargain, and would be left with 250 gallons surplus to be sold at a profit.

It is hoped that this example will provide a sufficient intuitive base for three generalizations, the rigorous proof of which would be too complex to enter into here. All of these generalizations concern a distinction between *internal* and *external* costs. By internal costs, we mean the value of resources used up directly in an act of production and consumption by the person doing the producing or consuming. By external costs, we mean the value of resources which are used up indirectly or inadvertently as a by-product of the act of production or consumption. (In the example which we have just discussed, the production of paper involved internal costs of 1/2 cent per pound, representing the value of the labor, machinery, and raw materials used up internally within the paper mill; and external costs of 1/4 cent per pound, representing the value of the labor, filtration devices, and chemicals which were used downstream in the water works to counteract the additional pollution of the water caused by the production of that pound of paper.)

The distinction between internal and external costs may be expressed in several other ways and seen in many other examples. For instance, we could distinguish internal costs as those which are imposed upon the person who initiates and directly benefits from the activity in question, and external costs as those which he imposes upon others. Consider a person who operates a noisy motorcycle. He himself bears the costs of gasoline, maintenance, depreciation, and so forth; but he succeeds in imposing part of the costs of operation on others when instead of spending money for a quieter muffler he makes others pay for soundproofing, tranquilizers, and sleeping pills—or just pay in nervous energy.

Another way to look at the distinction is to say that internal costs correspond to voluntary transactions, while external costs correspond to involuntary, forced transactions. When I buy a bottle of beer I engage in a voluntary transaction with the storekeeper, a two-way exchange in which I give him some money and he gives me the bottle. When I throw the empty bottle out of my car window onto your lawn I am forcing you to participate in a one-way, involuntary transaction—you give me the service of rubbish disposal, whether you want to or not, and I give you nothing in return.

Finally, we could classify as internal costs those which use up resources by setting in motion a chain of cause and effect which travels through the market system, and external costs as those which use up resources by setting off chains of cause and effect passing through the natural environment. When a farmer sprays his apple trees, he sets off chain reactions of both types. He uses the retailing services of his local supplier, who in turn uses the wholesale services of regional suppliers, who in turn draws on the productive capacity of a chemical plant, who in turn uses up labor and raw materials, the production of which necessitates the use of still other resources, and so on. The price of the insecticide represents the sum total of all the costs added up all along the line, and the farmer pays this as an internal cost of producing apples. But the use of pesticides also sets off other chains of cause and effect—the material washes off his trees into nearby streams, where it is eaten by little fish who concentrate it in their fatty tissues, and in turn swim downstream to be eaten by bigger fish who further concentrate the poison. These bigger fish are eaten by, among other creatures, the American bald eagle, who consequently lays eggs with soft shells or no shells at all, and is thus threatened with extinction. How much is an eagle worth? A man who illegally shoots one must pay a $500 fine for the privilege, but a farmer who poisons one as part of the external costs of growing apples pays nothing.

Now we come to the three generalizations concerning internal and external costs which were promised earlier. The first of these is that whenever external costs of production or consumption are present in an economy, the invisible hand of competition will, if unaided, fail as a guide to the efficient allocation of resources.

The second generalization, really a corollary of the first, is that whenever external effects of production or consumption exist, there will in principle exist some potential agreement among all parties concerned which will benefit at least one person and harm none of the others. This means, among other things, that whenever the external cost in question is a form of pollution, there exists some possible pollution abatement program benefiting *both* the perpetrator and the victims of the pollution.

The third generalization is that whenever an activity involves pollution, or the imposition of some other type of external cost, a *reduction* in that activity will almost always be part of any program to achieve an efficient allocation of the resources involved. If the production of steel, cement, or automobile transportation pollutes the air, we may be pretty sure that we should be using less of these and more, say, of aluminum, bricks, and electric railways.

How to Make Pollution Go Away

If pollution is such an undisputably bad thing, the reader may say, not only unpleasant and aesthetically offensive but inefficient and harmful to polluter and victim alike, then let's just get rid of it! Let's get the government to ban leaded gasoline, outlaw DDT, regulate the type of fuel used by Con Ed, require secondary treatment for all sewage, impose standards on atomic power stations, insist on chemical toilets on all pleasure boats, punish people who litter the highways, and control the phosphate content of detergents! After all, isn't that what the government is for—to ban, outlaw, regulate, require, impose, insist, punish, and control?

This seems to be the instinctive reaction of a great many Americans upset about the pollution problem. The politicians whom they send to our legislatures at regularly appointed intervals are only too happy to oblige—if this new public concern will give them a chance to control something which they do not yet control, or set up a bureau or regulatory commission where one does not yet exist, what intelligent politician would pass up the opportunity?

To succumb to the urge to control pollution via the imposition of direct controls out of the belief that these are quick, expedient, or effective ways of getting the job done, would, I believe, be a grave mistake. Instead, I would like to offer some guidelines for a more efficient, equitable, and effective pollution abatement policy.

The first guideline which I propose is to make minimum use of direct controls in fighting pollution, and maximum use of market mechanisms and the price system. To illustrate how this guideline might be applied in a specific case let us take the very important example of automobile exhaust pollution. This is, incidentally, an area in which direct controls are already being used in the form of requiring certain emission control devices on all cars produced in and imported into the United States. Other direct controls are pending, including regulation of permissible types of fuels, still more effective emission control devices, and the outright banning of automobile traffic from certain urban areas.

As an alternative to such proposals, I would argue in favor of controlling auto exhaust pollution by putting a price tag on the privilege to pollute. In our Capitalist economy you can impose upon me the inconvenience of work or the inconvenience of using my lawn as a parking lot only by paying a price, and if I do not judge the price to be high enough I am free to decline your offer. Why, then, should you be able to impose upon me the inconvenience of breathing the noxious gasses emitted from your exhaust pipe without paying a price, when, because of the simple physics of the situation, I don't even have the opportunity to refuse your offer to have me breathe them?

The idea of putting a price on exhaust emission at first may bring to mind the image of a little gadget like a water meter which would be clamped on the tailpipe of a car to be read once a month and a bill sent out, so much per cubic foot. If the construction of such a meter were practical, it would be an ideal method to use. As far as I know, this meter has not yet been developed, but a somewhat more primitive approach using existing institutions and technology could accomplish much the same purpose. For example, in a state like Vermont, which already requires a semiannual trip to the inspection station, the pollution charge could be combined with regular inspection. When a car was taken in, it would be rated according to an established scale of points. Starting with a basic score scaled to the engine displacement and mileage since the last inspection, so many points could be deducted for a P.C.V. system, and so many points for fuel injection, a catalytic muffler, and so on and so forth. At the end, a fee would be paid in proportion to the points remaining, which might range, let us imagine, from $100 for a massive Chrysler with no technical refinements down to $2.00 for a Volkswagen converted to run on natural gas.

Compared to the current system of direct controls, the price system would offer distinct advantages with respect to efficiency, equity, and incentives. Let us look at these advantages one by one.

The price system would be more efficient because it would

observe the equimarginal principle. If you are going to use up resources in a variety of related but not identical activities, you will get the greatest yield per unit expenditure by dividing your resources among the different activities in such a way that the benefit of spending an additional penny at the margin is the same for each activity.

This principle applies also to the control of automobile exhaust. The total amount of pollution control expenditure should be divided among individual cars in such a way that the marginal yield, measured in terms, say, of cubic feet of carbon monoxide reduction per dollar spent, would be the same for all cars.

Now, direct controls clearly violate this principle. The current law requires that some fixed sum—let us say about $10.00—be spent on every car for positive crankcase ventilation. In the case of a big car which is driven alot that $10.00 does a great deal of good. In the case of a little car, or a little used one, it does less good. Clearly, it would be more efficient to spend some of the money used on the little cars for still better control devices on big cars. Under the price system this would be done. A Buick-owning traveling salesman would probably get almost every device in the book before he got to the point where another dollar spent on technical refinements would not pay off in terms of reduced inspection tax, while the proverbial little old lady who drives her Renault once a week to church might find that even the most basic devices weren't worth putting on.

The second point of superiority of the price system lies in its equity. This has already been hinted at in our previous example—it is clearly equitable that the salesman pay more pollution tax than the little old lady. In addition to this aspect of equity, which makes people pay in proportion to the cost which they impose on others by pollution, there is another, almost reverse aspect. It is also equitable to allow people to pollute more in proportion to the benefit which they gain from pollu- tion! Compare two car owners, one of whom views his car just as a means of getting from place to place and the other for whom his car is his principle hobby and driving his chief source of amusement. The first man will be little inconvenienced by the slight reduction in perform- ance which is produced by the mandatory P.C.V. system. The second man, however, will be grievously annoyed when he finds that his zero to sixty acceleration time has risen from 9.6 seconds to 9.7. Would it not be more equitable to allow this second man to take his P.C.V. valve off, as long as he is willing to pay the increased inspection tax which will result and as long as that tax realistically reflects the cost which he imposes upon others by so doing?

Finally, the price system for exhaust emission control would be superior to the direct control system with respect to its incentive value. This must already be clear in general terms, but let us add a few specifics. It must be pointed out that under the current system there is no incentive whatsoever for the car owner to *maintain* pollution control devices installed by law on his car. Here we are not just worried about the hot rodder who purposely takes the thing off to get that extra edge of performance. More significantly, how many car owners even *know* that the Rochester valve of the P.C.V. system must be replaced every 10,000 miles or the system is rendered useless? And of those who do know this, how many are tempted to save the dollar or two a year involved by just letting the matter slide?

Furthermore, in the matter of incentives it is not so much the car owner as the car manufacturer who counts. The present system by insisting that every car maker, domestic and foreign, be treated exactly equally guarantees that no manufacturer can get a competitive advantage by producing a more pollution-free car. In fact, the situation is if anything the exact opposite. If the manufacturer is going to act rationally in his own self-interest to maximize his profits, it will pay him to spend millions not in the research laboratories but in the lobbies of Congress fighting pollution control legislation tooth and nail! There is much talk about a "conspiracy" of the big three to suppress technical developments which could reduce pollution. Maybe there is a conspiracy and maybe there isn't, but how long do you think one could last against the competition of Volkswagen, Fiat, and Toyota if the annual pollution charge paid by the owner for an American car was triple that for their foreign competitors? Let's take the profit out of pollution and put it into pollution *control,* then we'll get a real look at the Capitalist economy in action.

There are a few signs on the horizon that the price system for pollution control may be gaining favor. For automobiles, President Nixon's tax on the lead additive in gasoline appears to be a small step in the right general direction. The system has been widely suggested for control of water pollution also, where the metering of wastes is more practical. A similar system is already in use in the Ruhr Valley in Germany, and pilot programs are underway in this country. The possibilities have still not been fully explored. How about, for example, a differential charge for garbage collection in the city according to whether noisy metal cans or quiet plastic ones are used? How about a differential liquor tax on beer according to whether the product is sold in indestructible aluminum cans or biodegradable plastic containers?

All of the pricing schemes mentioned so far have one drawback in common in that they require initiative to be taken by the government to put them into effect, and administration and regulation by bureaucratic government agencies. As long as cleaning up pollution is left to the politicians there is grave danger that whatever Federal Pollution Control Commission is set up will go the way of the FCC, the FDA, the ICC, the CAB, and virtually all other federal, state, and local regulatory and licensing agencies. In case after case the ordinary citizen has seen that regulators quickly become tools of those whom they supposedly regulate. Corruption and the protection of special interests creep in, and public service drops to last priority.

For this reason, I will propose a second guideline, namely that whenever possible the price system for pollution control should be instituted *not* by administrative means but by modifications of our legal system and the extension of the property rights of individuals.

Property rights are a part of our social system which, if they are to be justified at all, must be justified on the grounds that they induce socially beneficial behavior. Our private property system in this country, like almost all other aspects of our economic system, was developed in the 19th century, a time when, at least in the wide-open continent of America, the throughput economy model was not such a wildly inaccurate picture of the world as it is today. In the throughput economy of the 19th century the most important socially beneficial behavior which was stimulated by the private property system was the function of asset creation (capital formation, saving, or whatever you want to call it) that led to economic growth. Now that we live in the spaceship earth of the late 20th century we know that the path to the good life no longer lies through the brute force method of asset creation alone. Instead, we must learn to economize on the use of sources and sinks which we once thought limitless, and learn to recycle our wastes. What is the matter with our laws and property rights, and how can they be modified to suit the new conditions? I will give just two examples.

In the first, let us look at water pollution again. A great American industrialist is reputed to have said that the ability of our rivers and streams to carry sewage off to the ocean is one of our great natural resources. He couldn't have been more correct! These great natural sewers must surely have contributed as much to American economic development as our vast ore and coal fields, the great wheatlands, or the forests of the Northwest. But the exploitation of timber, cropland, and mineral rights, although undergoing some terribly wasteful phases in the last century when these were treated virtually as free goods, has now been brought under fairly rational control by the simple fact that each unit of these resources is the private property of some individual or business corporation. If you want to cut down a tree, you are going to have to pay the owner, so you don't do it unless you really need that wood and can't use a substitute. The same goes for corn, steel, oil, or anything else. Yet our great natural sewers are the property of no one! Since no one has any property rights in them, who is going to guard against their destruction? Who is going to charge for their use? Small wonder we are a hundred years behind on water pollution control.

What could be done to save the situation within the framework of the property system? A really radical proposal would be for the federal government to put all the nation's major rivers and lakes up for auction, and let the highest bidders regulate and economize on their use. If General Motors owned the Mississippi River, it would surely charge for the privilege of dumping in it, and would presumably also consider bids for conservation groups and communities to keep parts of it clean for bathing and fishing.

A less radical proposal than actually creating property rights in the rivers would be to create property rights in the right to pollute itself. It has been suggested that the government auction off a certain number of certificates, fixed once and for all, each giving the right to dump so many thousands of cubic feet of waste. These certificates would then become the property of their owners, to be bought and sold at will. They would end up in the hands of those industries where pollution control was most technically difficult and expensive, and other industries would move or clean up rather than pay the price of a certificate.

The second example for pollution control via the law of property has to do with the obscure corner of the legal system known as the law of nuisance. In our system property ownership includes the right to use free from outside interference, as well as the obligation to use in such a way as not to injure others. Unfortunately, our system for enforcing the first right is faulty. Our laws work pretty well in the area of private nuisance. If you build a barbeque in your back yard, and the smoke blows over and ruins the flavor of the cupcakes baked in the bakery next door, chances are you will be sued and have to pay damages. These damage payments, or the threat of them, put a price on pollution for you and deter you from building the barbeque or using it as often as you otherwise would.

In the area of law known as public nuisance, however, the system does not work nearly as well. If the previous example is changed so that you are building a steel mill, and causing damage not only to your neighbor but to all the inhabitants of a forty-mile radius, you might imagine that the threat of suit and the imposition of damages would be still greater than before. But it is less! This is because only an agency of the government is empowered to sue for public nuisance. An individual cannot initiate a suit unless he can show special damages concentrated upon him alone (for example, the bakery might be able to sue the steel mill). It is as if the law allowed you to defend yourself against a mugger who attacked only you, but did nothing to help if he robbed just a little from everyone in your neighborhood!

The problem is very similar to that in some areas of consumer protection law. If General Motors builds a defective car an individual can, under the proper conditions, sue the company to recover damages to himself. A few such cases will do little to compel the company to build safer cars, since the damages in each case will be small. To solve the problem it has been suggested that the law be modified to allow an individual to bring what is called a "class suit," a suit requiring payment of damages to himself and to all others similarly damaged, however many thousands of these there may be. The threat of class suits, it is hoped, will deter companies from making shoddy products.

The class suit principle could also be brought to bear in the area of pollution, by modifying the law to allow an individual to bring a class suit against the perpetrator of a public nuisance. This would be an enormously powerful deterrent to industrial pollution. Imagine that just one of the residents of the lower stretches of a river were able to bring a suit against a large polluter upstream for the total sum of damages to all residents! This would certainly put a high price tag on pollution and the company would be forced to shut down, clean up, or compensate the damaged parties for the violation of their property rights.

As in the case of emission and effluent charges there are a few hopeful signs of progress in reforming the legal system to help control pollution. The State of Michigan, for example, has recently passed and signed into law a measure that will allow a citizen to file suit against anyone, including the state itself, believed to be seriously contaminating the air, water, or land resources belonging to all. This is obviously a step in the right direction. It has the drawback, from the economist's point of view, of not providing for the payment of damages to injured parties but only permitting the court to grant injunctions, impose conditions, or direct the upgrading of standards for the polluter, and thus of simply transferring the problems of direct controls from the executive to the judicial branches of government. Nonetheless, it has the enormous advantage of allowing the injured party, the private citizen, to take the initiative against major polluters without being subject to the quick brush-off or the endless delay which are the twin traits of administrative bureaucracy.

chapter 4

THE POLITICAL ECONOMY OF
ECOLOGICAL ACTION

The Efficiency Paradox

In the last chapter, by application of elementary economic analysis, it was shown that pollution and all other types of economic activities which impose external costs on parties not voluntarily taking part in them are sources of inefficiency in the economy. When such external effects are present the price system fails to guide individuals in seeking satisfaction of their material desires exclusively in ways which benefit others at the same time (or at a minimum, leave others unharmed). In the latter part of the chapter several suggestions were made for restructuring the price system and the system of property rights so as to provide people with incentives for abandoning ecologically destructive modes of production and consumption.

In the course of this discussion the astute reader may have been puzzled by one problem. Why is it, he might ask, that we have to go to the trouble of rigging up some special, artificial system of incentives to control pollution? For isn't it true, by definition, that whenever an *inefficiency* exists in the economy there must also exist at least one way of reallocating resources which would leave at least one individual better off and no one worse off? And if such an opportunity exists, will it not be immediately taken advantage of by the potential beneficiary or beneficiaries, while all other parties maintain an attitude of benign non-intervention? Won't all problems of pollution, then, except perhaps those resulting from irrational malice and ignorance, eventually be taken care of spontaneously through voluntary negotiation among the parties concerned?

These are very interesting questions indeed. Here is an apparent paradox, which we will refer to as the "efficiency paradox." It cannot easily be resolved within the realm of pure economic theory, where human and nonhuman economic resources appear only as abstract pawns pushed around on an n-dimensional chessboard by an invisible hand linked to an omniscient brain. We must venture into the flesh-and-blood world of political economy, where every economic decision, every reallocation of resources entails not only a readjustment of material relations among things but at the same time of social relations among men.

This chapter will be devoted to exploring some elementary principles of political economy which can help us explain why it is that when individuals have opportunities for securing pure mutual benefit they are not always observed to take advantage of them.

Who Should Pay for the Cleanup?

Although pure economc theory tries as much as possible to avoid normative considerations—those involving such human values as justice, equity, and fair play, where standards may vary widely from individual to individual—in the real world normative considerations cannot be ignored. They often play a crucial role in the making of resource allocation decisions, and we can take the first step toward resolution of the efficiency paradox by introducing one of these normative questions—who should pay for the cleanup?

Suppose that in a certain small community a chemical processing plant is emitting a strong, evil odor which pervades the entire town. It is always difficult to put a cash value on the damage caused in such a case, but, judging by the amount of money people spend to pamper their nostrils with deodorants, perfumes, aerosols, incense, and flowers, let us conservatively assume that each of the 1000 residents of this community would think it a bargain to be rid of the nuisance for as little as $10. Suppose further that the cost of scrubbing and filtering equipment at the plant which would entirely suppress the odor is estimated at $6000. What is to be done?

Clearly, the analysis of Chapter 3 applies, and an opportunity for mutual beneficial action to remove the source of the inefficiency exists. Each citizen of the town could contribute $6 to a general fund, to present the factory owner with a big crate of scrubbing and filtering equipment. Each citizen would thus profit to the extent of $4 (since they would get rid of a $10 nuisance at the bargain price of $6), and the owner would have lost nothing.

From the point of view of pure economic theory this would be an excellent scheme, yet an obvious normative objection would surely arise in practice. Why, it would be said, should the citizens of the town pay any part of the cost of pollution abatement? Isn't the plant owner the one who is at fault? Isn't he the aggressor? Do not justice, equity, and fair play require that *he* bear the cost of cleaning up his establishment, and perhaps pay retroactive damages to the injured parties as well?

This is a powerful and persuasive line of argument, and it goes a long way toward resolving our paradox; for it says that the path of voluntary mutual accommodation, which always exists as a theoretical possibility in the case of any inefficiency, may sometimes be morally unacceptable. To follow this path would seem to many like bargaining with a mugger who has just clubbed you and stolen your billfold, to give him your watch as well in return for a promise not to hit you a second time.

Yet once the path of mutual accommodation is abandoned, the community is divided into two warring factions, and the propollution faction may win the ensuing political struggle. This is particularly true since the factory owner is not likely to be without allies. If he has to clean up he may pass part of the cost along to his customers in the form of a price increase, so his customers may testify on his behalf before the city council. If less of the product can be sold at the higher price, he may have to lay off some of his workers, and thus his employees may join the propollution faction.

The addition of these allies does not alter the normative analysis of the situation, for if the act of pollution itself is a crime then these allies are nothing but partners in crime. The customers of the firm are in a position analytically identical to the recipient of stolen goods. The producer kept his price low only by forcing the residents adjacent to his establishment involuntarily to subsidize the cost of production, by permitting their lungs and noses to be used as industrial waste disposal units, substituting for the mechanical units which should have been installed at the plant. The customers no more deserve to benefit from this tactic than does the owner himself.

The employees of the chemical plant are in no better position. When the boss of a crime syndicate is captured and jailed, do we care for the scores of his henchmen, flunkies, and bodyguards who are forced to seek alternative employment?

It should be mentioned as a theoretical possibility that if every single one of the members of our hypothetical community benefited from the chemical plant as either customer or employee, then the way might be reopened to seek a solution through voluntary mutual accommodation. Except in this extreme case it is certain that those who bear the costs of pollution without receiving any of the benefits of production will object to making any contribution to pollution abatement, saying that no one, owner, shareholder, customer, worker, or city councilman has a right to make his living at the expense of innocent bystanders.

As a final note it should be emphasized that our analysis provides no reason why the consumers of a product, the price of which has been kept artificially low by passing on part of its cost to pollution victims, should not bear at least part of the cost of pollution abatement. Although this seems self-evident the opposition opinion is occasionally voiced. I have heard people complain that if strict automobile emission standards were imposed, the giant corporations which manufacture our cars would be able to pass the cost of installing the necessary emission control devices on to their customers by raising prices. This not only would but *should* happen. Disposing of waste products is just as much a part of the cost of operating a car as buying gasoline and tires, and in the natural course of things we should expect it to be borne by the car owner.

Some Problems of Organizing Collective Action

The pollution abatement suggestions of Chapter 3 all promoted *individual* action for improving the habitability of our environment. The incentives provided would help harmonize economic decisions taken by producers and consumers acting independently, thus promoting economic efficiency and ecological rationality. Some other proposals for pollution abatement and environmental improvement are based not on the principle of individual but of *collective* action. Whenever a group of people are faced with a common environmental problem, suggestions will always be heard that the members of the group should in some way cooperate in pursuing their common interest. In many, if not all cases, even programs like those of Chapter 3, which depend on the principle of individual action for their ongoing operation, may require some sort of collective action to put them into effect in the first place, for example, passing new legislation or repealing old. The problems of organizing individuals to act collectively are of particular interest to the ecological economist, as we will see.

As our situational paradigm let us choose a community suffering from objectionable fumes emanating from fires in an abandoned mine on the edge of town, dug years ago by a company long since bankrupt and out of existence. (Situations much like this exist in many of the old coal mining districts of this country.) Clearly, in contrast to the conditions of our previous example, the possibility of imposing the cost of pollution abatement on those parties which caused the trouble in the first place simply does not exist. Assume a total cleanup bill of $6,000 and a total damage, at $10 per head, of $10,000.

In principle, it would be a good idea to put out the fires and seal off the mine shafts. However, some form of collective action is plainly required to accomplish this, since no individual, acting on his own, is going to put up the whole $6,000 to reap $10 worth of benefits. Not only would it be unprofitable for any individual to undertake the entire project for his own benefit but also it would seem very difficult for a group of citizens to band together and form a corporation to undertake the project as a commercial venture (as might happen if the community needed, say, a new water supply). Because it would not be possible to exclude any member of the community from the benefits of the project once it were carried out, there would be no way to sell the benefits to individuals; all would receive the "product" whether they paid or not.

The mine cleanup project proposed is what economists call a *public good*. Because separate individuals cannot be excluded from enjoying the benefits if they are produced for anyone at all, and because the cost is large relative to the benefits accruing to any one individual, it is generally held that such goods cannot be supplied by individual action within the framework of the market but must be provided, if at all, by some type of collective action.

Organizing a group of people to supply a public good is a task fraught with pitfalls. Every effort to secure the cooperation of individuals in working together for the common good stumbles against the famous *free rider problem*. Although every individual would benefit if he, together with all the others, acted cooperatively to secure the public good, he would benefit *still more* if everyone else worked together to provide the good in question, while he secured the benefit of their effort (from which he cannot, *ex hypothesi,* be excluded) and acted as a free rider. This "let George do it" attitude, which seems to be deeply engrained in human nature, causes no end of difficulty whenever an attempt is made to organize collective action; for if everyone tries to act as a free rider at once, obviously nothing will be accomplished.

It should be noted that the free rider problem occurs in a somewhat wider variety of situations than that suggested by the mine-sealing example. It is likely to be present when efforts are made to organize collective action for preventing the production of a "public bad." It reduces the hopes, for example, of securing the voluntary agreement of all auto owners to install catalytic mufflers, of all campers to abstain from littering, of all beer drinkers to use returnable bottles or urge recycling, of all housewives to use low-phosphate detergents, or of all manufacturers to eliminate excess packaging, even though each of these agreements, were they to come about, might result in clear mutual benefits for all participants. But for this one stumbling block we might ultimately see the adoption of the "new ecological ethic" proposed as a solution to the environmental crisis by ecological evangelists.

The free rider problem is rooted in the tendency of the individual member of a group, when faced with the choice of whether or not to act in the general interest, to assume that the actions of others will not change regardless of his own decision. Suppose, for instance, that we have a lake which is polluted by raw sewage dumped into it from vacation cottages along its shores. If all property owners stopped polluting the lake the increase in its recreational value might compensate them far more than the expense of installing sewage treatment facilities. However, the question which each individual owner will put to himself is, "If all others continue to act as they are acting now, what should I do?" Weighing the considerable expense of treating his own sewage against the negligible benefit of reducing the pollution level of the lake by one one-hundredth or one-thousandth part, he will doubtless continue to pollute. If, by some yet unspecified means, everyone agreed to stop polluting, the same line of reasoning on the part of each individual would soon lead to a breakdown of the agreement. Each would reason that as long as the others *continue* to treat their sewage, the water will remain adequately clean even if he were to dump his own small contribution of raw effluent.

The analysis of the previous paragraph suggests that the free rider problem might be overcome by changing the characteristics of the situation for the individual in one of two ways. First, things can sometimes be arranged so that it will be worthwhile for the individual to act in the group interest even if others do *not* follow his example. Second, it is sometimes possible to rig the situation in such a way that it will *not* be reasonable for the individual to assume that the behavior of others will continue uninfluenced by his own decision. Let us consider each of these possibilities.

The first possible escape from the free rider problem may arise spontaneously if the group in question is sufficiently small. Suppose that the polluted body of water we are considering is a very small pond on which there are only two cottages. In this situation it may well be that each cottage owner will consider the benefit of reducing total pond pollution by fifty percent to be sufficient to justify the expense of installing his own sewage treatment equipment, even if his neighbor does not do likewise. While it is not certain that exactly the optimal amount of sewage treatment equipment will be installed under these circumstances, at least it is likely that some steps will be taken in the right direction.

Generally speaking, the larger the group, the less likely it is that individuals will see it to their own advantage to act in the common interest. However, some techniques have been suggested to extend the applicability of this principle to larger groups. One is to form an organization which simultaneously acts to pursue the common interests of the group and to provide separate benefits to individual members. An example of such an organization in the environmental field is the Sierra Club. This organization carries out activities, such as lobbying for the expansion of National Parks, which are in the common interest of all conservationists. If this were all the organization did, however, it would be difficult to hold together, for nonmember, free-riding conservationists would benefit as much as members, and not have to contribute time or money to the work of the club. To hold on to its membership, the organization provides other services as well, such as distributing publications, organizing outings, and so on for its members only. It thus pays the individual to join, if only to secure these private benefits not availble to the free rider, and in doing so, he promotes the common interest of the group as well.

The alternative method of avoiding the free rider problem, that of convincing the individual group member that others' actions are not independent of his own, may also arise naturally in sufficiently small groups. Suppose that in either the lake pollution or the mine sealing examples, the total number of individuals involved were large enough so that no one would undertake to defend the common interest on his own, yet small enough so that all were acquainted and came into frequent contact. Suppose further that an informal agreement were made to share the expense of the cleanup among members of the group. It is much more likely that this agreement would be respected than if the group were larger, for now the individual participant will no longer be able to assume that no one would notice if he dropped out to become a free rider. Each party to the agreement will very likely fear that if he sets a bad example by failing to fulfill his share of the mutual obligation, others will follow his lead and the group will soon be back to the less preferable initial situation.

Occasionally this method of circumventing the free rider problem may also be extended to larger groups. One way to do this is somehow to formalize the understanding that continued participation of others will depend on the continued participation of oneself. If our lake had one hundred cottages along its shores a petition might be circulated under the terms of which each signer would pledge to desist from polluting, but only on the condition that at least fifty others agreed to do the same. Assuming that the pledge could be made legally binding, a property owner would be more willing to sign it than to undertake individual action, for in case the quota were not met he would lose nothing at all, and if it were met, he would reap exactly the same benefit as was derived in the earlier example where there were only two cottages on the lake. It is entirely possible that 100 percent of the residents might be willing to sign this conditional pledge, even though none of them would sign an unconditional one to clean up regardless of what others did. This approach could also be successful in raising money to finance a public good, such as the mine-sealing project.

Democracy and Collective Economic Action

In the previous two sections we discovered that even when there are clear mutual gains to be had from agreeing to carry out collectively a program of environmental amelioration, some very sticky normative and organizational problems may make it difficult or impossible to achieve the necessary degree of cooperation by voluntary means. With the prospects for voluntary collective action so limited and uncertain, it is small wonder that one often hears proposals to slice the Gordian knot by dropping the requirement that such action must be organized voluntarily. Wouldn't it be much more straightforward and effective in situations like those of our examples simply to coerce everyone into joining a nonvoluntary organization to serve the common interest? Since such proposals are so frequently met with and so frequently put into effect, we must devote a little space to exploring the merits of nonvoluntary collective action as a means of achieving our common interest in rational and efficient use of the environment.

In discussing nonvoluntary collective action we will limit ourselves to cases where the government provides the framework for organizing the action, and to those possible forms of governmental organizations in which government decisions are made by democratic vote of the citizens of the community in question. We will consider first whether decision making on the basis of democratic voting, with the minority bound to the decisions of the majority, provides a means for attaining economic efficiency in the face of environmental problems, and second whether majority rule conforms with the normative standard suggested earlier, that individuals should not be able to force part of the costs of their own production or consumption activities on to others via the imposition of external effects or other means.

If we begin by analyzing the effects of majority rule in the very simple situations of our earlier examples it appears to be a very attractive approach to environmental decision making. Let us look first at the community which was suffering from the fumes of the abandoned mine. It is clear that if a proposal were put to a referendum to raise $6,000 for the project by a tax levied uniformly on the 1,000 citizens of the town, it would have no difficulty getting a majority of the votes. Since each individual would face the identical possibility of gaining a $10 share of the benefits in return for bearing a $6 share of the costs, it is very likely that the proposal could be approved unanimously. Neither approval nor implementation of the project would be hampered by the free rider problem, since free ridership could now occur only in the form of legally punishable tax evasion.

It is equally likely that the problem of lake pollution could be solved by proposing a measure for referendum which would directly prohibit dumping raw sewage into the water. Again, each property

owner would see that his share of the benefits would exceed his share
of the costs, and that no free riders would be permitted.

The obvious equity and efficiency of the majority rule principle
as applied in these examples naturally raises the hope that it may offer
a way out of our troubles in a very wide variety of situations. Unfortunately, these hopes turn out to be largely unfounded, for the smooth
functioning of the democratic decision-making process in these examples is a result of two special features and is not generally characteristic of the problems encountered in the real world. One of these
features is that the benefits of the proposed project accrue in exactly
equal proportion to each member of the community in our examples.
The other is that we have considered the projects as if they called
for all-or-nothing decisions, without the possibility of intermediate
measures.

Suppose that we remove these special features from one of our
examples and see what happens. In the mining town let us imagine that
the opening from which the fumes emanate is not on the edge of town
but within the city limits. Four hundred citizens live to the west of this
opening, and the remaining six hundred to the east. The wind blows
from the west twice as often as from the east, so that the damage
suffered by the western residents is only $5 apiece, while the damage
suffered by easterners remains $10 apiece as before. To further alter the
situation, let us assume that existing technology allows not only for
all-or-nothing control of the fumes but also for any partial degree of
control which may be desired. As is the case in a great many economic
undertakings, we will imagine that fume control at this mine is subject
to some such scale of increasing marginal cost as that shown in Table
4.1. To reduce the emissions by 1 percent may at first be very inexpen-
sive, but further 1 percent reductions become increasingly costly.

Suppose that all 1,000 citizens of this community gather together
in a town meeting to listen to fume control proposals and vote on them.
At first someone might make the modest proposal that emissions be
reduced by 1 percent. The city engineer, called upon to speak, might
inform the assembled citizens that the cost of this proposal would be $1.
Each easterner, perceiving that he would reap a benefit worth 10¢ to
him from a 1 percent reduction in fumes and that his share of the tax
burden to support this project would be only 1/10¢, would decide to
vote for the project. The westerners would also approve of a 1 percent
reduction, getting a 5¢ benefit for 1/10¢ in taxes.

Before this motion were even brought to a vote, an amendment could be offered to increase the degree of control to 2 percent. Consulting the table we can see that this would increase the total cost by $1 more, and again both easterners and westerners would approve.

TABLE 4.1 Hypothetical cost schedule for fume reduction

Percent reduction	Total cost (in dollars)	Marginal cost (in dollars)
1	1	
2	2	1
3	5	3
4	10	5
5	17	7
—		9
—	—	—
—	—	—
—	—	—
24	530	—
25	577	47
26	626	49
27	677	51
—	—	—
—	—	—
—	—	—
49	2305	—
50	2402	97
51	2501	99
52	2602	101
—	—	—
—	—	—
99	9605	—
100	9802	197

Continuing in this fashion, the meeting might unanimously approve fume control up to 26 percent. However, with the next proposal, to raise the control level from 26 to 27 percent, the atmosphere of the meeting would suddenly change. From our table, we see that the marginal cost has now risen to $51. This would be fine for the easterners, who would each gain an additional 10¢ benefit at the expense of a 5.1¢ increment in taxes, but what about the westerners? Their 5¢ marginal benefit from this measure is now below the marginal cost to them of sharing the additional expense, so they would vote against it! When the proposal comes to a vote, the tally turns out to be 600 in favor, 400 opposed, and the meeting progresses to the next proposal, to move from 27 to 28 percent.

The next change in the voting occurs when the 51 percent control level is reached. When the suggestion is made to move on to 52 percent it is discovered that the additional tax burden per citizen of 10.1¢ is greater than the benefit even to the easterners. This next proposal, then, will not get a single vote, and the meeting will adjourn, having reached a final decision to reduce fume emission from the abandoned mine by a total of 51 percent.

Although the town meeting just described may perfectly exemplify participatory democracy, government by consent of the governed, majority rule, and many other sacred and glorious American political principles, its performance must nonetheless be rated as very poor by the standards which we have been employing. The same normative objection applies to the decision reached by the meeting as was discussed in the second section of this chapter. Some individuals (the easterners) are enjoying the benefits, part of the cost of which is imposed on others (the westerners) against their will, just as in our previous example, the polluting producer imposed part of his cost on the residents near his factory. The only difference lies in the mechanism by which the costs are involuntarily imposed on the nonbeneficiaries. In the one case, the costs were transferred by means of pollution, and in the other, by means of taxation.

Normative objections aside, the 51 percent cleanup decision reached by the town meeting is not even efficient. The origin of the inefficiency is easy to see. Each citizen, in deciding whether or not to vote for an increase in pollution control, weighed marginal benefits received against marginal costs imposed. Applying the equimarginal principle, the westerners would have liked only a 26 percent abatement program, while the easterners, applying the same reasoning, opted for 51 percent. Thus, under the system of majority rule governing the meeting, it was inevitable that the majority coalition of easterners, each applying the equimarginal principle to maximize his own net advantage, would force the westerners involuntarily to violate that same principle!

Looking at the matter another way, we can easily apply our standard efficiency test to the 51 percent decision, by seeing if its implementation would still leave room for a further mutually beneficial agreement among the townspeople. Such potential agreement does indeed turn out to exist. Simply consider the effect of cutting back pollution control from 51 to 50 percent. The easterners would each lose 10¢ in benefits, partially compensated for by a reduction of 9.9¢ in taxes, for a net loss of 0.1¢ each, or a grand total of 60¢ for the whole group. Each westerner, on the other hand, would lose a 5¢ benefit, but would be more than compensated by the 9.9¢ tax reduction, ending up with a net gain of 4.9¢, or a total of $19.60 for all westerners combined. Clearly, all parties would gain if the westerners banded together and offered a collective cash payment of somewhere between $.60 and $19.60 to the easterners, in return for a cutback to 50 percent pollution control. A series of such deals could in principle be negotiated until the degree of pollution control had been cut to 41 percent. (The reader might wish to verify as an exercise that at this point, where total marginal costs to all parties just equal total marginal benefits, an efficient degree of pollution control is reached, and that no further mutually beneficial agreements are possible.)

It is relatively unlikely that the series of deals just described could actually be carried out in practice, since any attempt to carry them out would encounter all of the by now familiar normative and organizational difficulties characteristic of voluntary collective action. It would be much more likely that the inequitable and inefficient 51 percent decision would be the one actually put into effect.

This somewhat lengthy example of the town meeting illustrates a very important general principle—that democratic voting is not an efficient method of making resource allocation decisions. This principle applies with particular force to decisions concerning public projects which confer special, differential benefits on a portion of the population and which are financed out of taxes levied on beneficiaries and non-beneficiaries alike.

In our example the misallocation of resources was in the direction of overfunding the project. Although the voting process might, in theory, also result in underfunding (suppose that in our example the westerners had been in the majority), there is reason to believe that in a complex representative democracy, like that of the United States, over-funding of public projects is more likely to be the case. Overfunding occurs when those parties receiving the largest benefits exert the strongest influence in the decision of the level at which the project is to be carried out. At least three factors favor the occurrence of this situation even when the beneficiaries may be numerically a minority of the population. First, since benefits are very often concentrated and highly prominent, while the costs of any one project are widely diffused and thus barely noticeable to the individual taxpayer, legislative representatives are apt to discover that voters pay more attention to the visible benefits than the invisible costs when deciding which way to vote in the next election. Second, a group of potential beneficiaries, if few in number and especially if already belonging to an ongoing interest-related organization, may easily be able to act collectively in lobbying for a given project, while the multitude of nonbeneficiaries, for all the reasons discussed above, may not be able to act together to thwart it. Finally, various types of legislative vote-trading—particularly those known as logrolling and porkbarreling—often make it possible to tie together several special-interest projects into a package deal acceptable to a majority of legislators.

For these reasons the legislative output of a representative government typically takes the form of a large number of special programs, each one of which benefits one minority group at the expense of the general public, and each one of which, taken separately, is overfunded. This fact is of profound importance for ecological economics, for it means that democratically-organized collective action for improvement of the environment may be liable to *precisely the same normative and economic objections as are the acts of pollution and environmental destruction which they are meant to counteract,* namely, 1. that the result of such action is to confer benefits on some at the expense of costs borne involuntarily by others and 2. that as a result of such action scarce economic and environmental resources are subject to inefficient and wasteful misallocation!

Is there no way in which we as citizens can act together, within the framework of our institutions of government, to cope with the environmental crisis? Fortunately, one type of governmental action is free from these objections—if that action is the adoption of a measure which corrects a situation in which some individual or individuals previously forced part of the costs of production or consumpton off on others by means of environmental externalities. If the offenders are made to pay the full costs themselves, the result is not to institute a new inefficiency but to remove an old one, and not to initiate a fresh inequity but to terminate one which has unjustly been permitted to exist in the past. The reader will find that all of the recommendations for the enactment or repeal of legislation at the federal, state, or local level which I recommend in this book fall into this category.

Unfortunately, the likelihood of existing institutions of democratic government adopting measures of this type and limiting themselves to these alone is rather small. We have seen that even the direct, participatory democracy of a town meeting can go astray in the field of environmental legislation. In the tangled jumble of representative bodies, administrative agencies, and regulatory commissions, where democracy fitfully struggles to function in the real world, the outlook is bleaker still. The opportunities for logrolling, porkbarreling, lobbying, favoritism, and corruption are sufficiently great that the political process all too often responds to the wishes of those who would destroy the environment at the expense of those who would benefit by its preservation, and all too often guards special interests and privileges more vigilantly than the general interest in maintaining economic efficiency and ecological rationality.

Yet to say that realism counsels pessimism provides no excuse for hiding one's head in the sand. A public aware of the basic principles of economics and ecology will surely see their environment degraded at a less rapid rate than if they were easy marks for duplicity and manipulation. It is with this modest educational aim in mind that this volume has been written.

chapter 5

Q. **COPING WITH THE POPULATION EXPLOSION** ?

A. STOP FUCKING A LOT.

What Are We in For?

There is an old story about a very wise man who invented a new game for the edification and amusement of his emperor—chess. The emperor was so delighted with the new pastime that he told the inventor to name his own reward, and he would receive it. "Sire," the man said, "I am a humble man of modest needs, and I ask only this: that you give me a single grain of wheat for the first square on the chessboard, two grains for the second square, four for the third, then eight, and so on until you have worked your way to the last square on the board."

The emperor at first insisted that the inventor take more than this, perhaps a bushel of gold coins or the pick of his harem, but when the man stuck to his original request the order was given for a servant to bring a jar of grain from the kitchen, and the counting began.

A single grain was placed on the first square, two on the second, then four, eight, sixteen, thirty-two . . . until, lo and behold, when the emperor reached the fourteenth square, counting out 8,192 grains, the jar which had been brought from the kitchen was emptied! A second jar was brought, but it sufficed only for the fifteenth square. Stubbornly, the emperor demanded that his kitchen be emptied, and all of his storehouse was wheeled in on a huge cart loaded with a thousand jars of wheat. Yet when the 8,388,608 grains required for the twenty-fourth square had been counted out, this cart too was emptied. At this point, the ruler, seeing what he was in for, called for the captain of his guard and gave the order that the wise inventor of the game of chess should be quietly garroted.[1]

This fable, like all such fables, has a moral: Playing around with runaway geometric progressions will get you in trouble sooner or later.

Let us see how this moral applies to the growth patterns of animate populations. Suppose we take a single yeast cell and place it on a culture dish (or take a pair of fruit flies and put them in a small cage, or a pair of dogs and put them on an island previously inhabited only by rabbits). Then, let us watch and see what happens to the population of the organism as time goes by.

At first the population will grow in simple geometric progression, like the grains on the chessboard. The biological characteristics of the species will determine some normal, fixed doubling time under optimal conditions, and the population will follow a path approximately like curve A in Figure 5.1.

Sooner or later, though, the population will begin to fill up its bottle or island or whatever, and the time needed to double the population in the more crowded conditions will increase. With fixed environmental limits the population curve will follow an S-shape like curve B in our figure. The deteriorating conditions for reproduction and survival as the population ceiling is approached eventually bring population growth to a complete halt.

Does this simple S-curve law of population growth apply to human populations as well? In the long run it surely does. In the short run, however—let us say over the period of the last two centuries—the curve of human population growth has departed from the normal S-

[1] And well he did so! To cover the board in the fashion suggested would have required no fewer than 18,446,744,073,709,551,615 grains of wheat, about a billion tons.

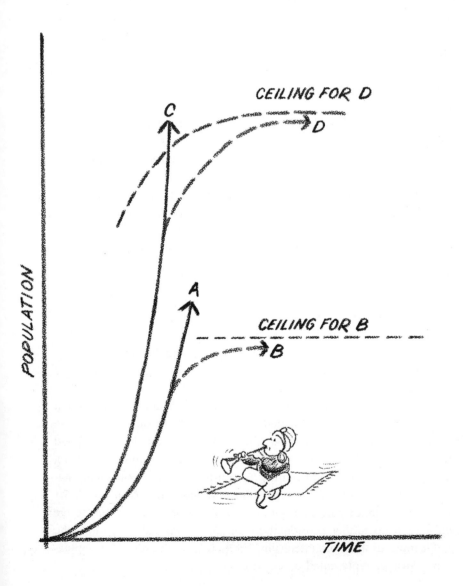

FIGURE 5.1   Hypothetical population growth curves

shape because of man's ability to alter his environment in certain ways which a fruit fly or yeast cell cannot do. In particular, principally because of advances in medical science, the human population has not been subjected to a fixed doubling time but to a steadily shortening one. The world population is now doubling about once every thirty-five years. The last doubling took about eighty years, the one before that some two hundred, and earlier ones longer still. To put it another way, not only has the human population grown but the rate of its growth has grown also.

No less significantly, advances in agricultural and industrial technology have effectively increased the size of the globe over the last two centuries, in terms of the maximum population which it will support.

Taken together, these two factors have so far kept the curve of human population growth from reaching the point where it would bend over to make an S-shape. What will the future bring? Some optimistic souls think that the curve will just keep going right on up like curve C in the figure. It has been estimated that the earth alone could accommodate twenty million times its present population, living at 120 per square meter in a 2000-story building covering the entire earth. It would take us 890 years, at our present rate of growth, to get to that point, and by then we may have solved the formidable technical and economic problems of interstellar travel, and be able to export our surplus to the stars (assuming the natives will supply us with the requisite number of immigrant visas).[2]

If people want to believe in this sort of thing there is no rational argument which can be presented to convince them otherwise. If one were to "prove" that it is impossible to travel faster than the speed of light and reach the stars, they could legitimately counter by citing "proofs" by eminent 19th-century scientists that heavier-than-air machines could never fly. For the present, however, curve C of Figure 5.1 lies in the realm of pure speculation, not of reasoned discussion, so we will give it no further consideration but go on instead to explore the implications of the more interesting alternative for the future of population growth as represented by curve D.

[2] The 2000-story building, space flight, and many other fascinating topics are discussed in a very worthwhile book compiled by Garrett Hardin: *Population, Evolution, and Birth Control*, 2nd ed. (San Francisco: W. H. Freeman and Company, 1969).

Curve D shows what would happen if we were to exhaust the technological possibilities for further raising the population ceiling. As the ceiling stops rising, and the population curve approaches it, the latter would necessarily bend over and assume the standard S-shape. Eventually, a condition of population equilibruim would be established, in which births just equaled deaths and each generation just reproduced itself.

Simply to say that a finite ceiling to population growth dictates an eventual approach to population equilibrium is not quite enough, for there is more than one way to achieve population equilibrium. The first type of equilibrium, beloved of the classical economists, is what we can call the marginal subsistence solution. Imagine a society for which there is some fixed population ceiling dictated by existing, fixed technology. Suppose that the reproductive behavior of the populace is such that each generation more than reproduces itself, consumer goods are available only via purchase, and income is not distributed equally over all members of society. As population grows, given the fixed technology, it is reasonable to assume that the prices of living space and food will rise relative to wages. Eventually, the poorest classes of society will be so disadvantaged by the rising cost of living that their conditions for reproduction and survival will be adversely affected. (Perhaps their birth rate will fall because of crowding, or their death rate will rise because of disease and malnutrition.) In any event, population growth ceases for these poorest classes, lowering the average for society as a whole. As population grows still more (at its now diminished rate), the next most prosperous group of families is pushed to the subsistence level. At the same time the first group may be expected to fall below the subsistence minimum, that is, to be pushed to such depths of poverty that deaths exceed births among them. The average population growth rate thus drops still further. In this way the margin of subsistence is pushed higher up the income ladder so that eventually excess births among the prosperous are just balanced by excess deaths among the destitute, and equilibrium is achieved.

This marginal subsistence solution to population growth was the "dismal theorem" advanced by T. R. Malthus in his famous book, *An Essay on the Principle of Population*. Its picture of a society in which affluence can exist only against the backdrop of miserable masses whose numbers are continuously replenished by the excess children of the rich driven down into poverty is indeed dismal.

Yet there exists a second type of population equilibrium more dismal still. We can call this the absolute subsistence solution. Suppose that the society which we are considering is the same as before, except that certain essential consumer goods—a minimum of food, clothing, and shelter—are available not solely via purchase but also, for those too poor to buy them, from public stocks purchased through taxation and distributed free of charge. Now, as population grows and prices rise, the lowest economic strata of society, rather than sinking below the subsistence level, simply make greater and greater use of public soup kitchens. As the number of clients of these increases, and as the price of the provender distributed rises, the burden of taxation placed upon the prosperous grows ever larger, accelerating *their* slide into poverty. All the while population growth continues, until eventually a situation is reached when everyone is patronizing the soup kitchens. At this point the opportunities for taxation are obviously exhausted, so the relief recipients themselves must go to work to produce their own rations. Eventually, when these rations are barely sufficient to give the strength needed for communal food production, the toilers returning home at the end of the day too tired and hungry to reproduce at a rate higher than the death rate, population equilibrium will be achieved.

Kenneth Boulding has called this line of reasoning the "utterly dismal theorem," for the only result of the charity designed to assuage Malthusian misery is ultimately to increase the sum total of human pain and suffering.

It should be noted that a dynamic variant of both the marginal and absolute subsistence solutions is possible. If we allow for *some* technological advance, but only enough to raise the population ceiling at a rate less rapid than the growth rate of population implicit in the reproductive behavior of well-fed members of society, a situation occurs in which either the dismal or the utterly dismal configuration is reproduced each year on a somewhat larger scale. Only if the rate of technological progress is sufficient to outrun population will things get better, given the assumptions we have been using. This is exactly what happened in Malthus' England for the next two hundred years or so following the publication of his book. But remember that we can't count on the *indefinite* continuation of such a rate of technological progress.

Is our only choice between the dismal and the utterly dismal? No, not quite. A third possibility exists, at least in principle, of a nonsubsistence solution. Suppose that something happened to bring the birth rate and death rate of a society into equality at a higher-than-subsistence standard of living. There are many ways in which this possibility might come to pass. A fad of celibacy or homosexuality might sweep the nations of the world. The frequency and ferocity of wars might increase. Esthetic and cultural standards might spontaneously become biased against large families. Increased use of herbicides, pesticides, and peaceful atomic energy might bring about an increased incidence of sterility and fatal birth defects. The Pharaoh might send around his troops to slaughter every eldest male child. The possibilities are endless, if not all equally attractive. Is there any chance that one of them might come to pass? We will investigate the prospects for our own country in the remainder of this chapter, and for developing nations in the next.

The Not-So-Simple Arithmetic of Population Growth

Anyone who has read *The Population Bomb* [3] is familiar with the simple arithmetic of population growth. To calculate the rate of population growth in a given country in a given year, you find the Crude Birth Rate (CBR, the number of babies born per 1000 of population in the given year), subtract from that the Crude Death Rate (CDR, the number of deaths per 1000 of population in the given year), and divide by ten to express the result as a percentage. For example, in Costa Rica in the late fifties, the Crude Birth Rate was 47.7 per 1000 and the Crude Death Rate was 9.6 per 1000, so that the Rate of Natural Increase of Population (RNI) was $47.7 - 9.6 = 38.1$ per 1000, or 3.81 percent per annum. For the same period in Luxembourg the figures were $15.9 - 11.9 = 4.0$, or .04 percent per annum.

The next lesson in population arithmetic comes with the translation of population growth rates expressed in percentage terms to population growth rates expressed as doubling times. A population which kept up the rate reported above for Costa Rica over a sustained period would double every 18 years. The doubling time for the population of Luxembourg would be a comfortable 173 years at the 0.4 percent rate. It's a good thing for Luxembourg, too, since the population density there is already a solid 123 per square kilometer!

On the basis of this much population arithmetic, we can have all sorts of fun and games. Remember the chess board? If Costa Rica kept growing at its present rate until the year 2100, its population would increase from its 1961 population of 1,225,000 to 250 million, about the population of the Soviet Union today. These people would be packed

---

[3] Paul R. Ehrlich, New York: Ballantine Books, 1968.

in no fewer than 4800 per square kilometer, compared with a mere 3000 or so per square kilometer in today's Hong Kong, the present record holder. If the 317,000 people of Luxembourg had been the only inhabitants of the world in the fourth century B.C., and had increased their population at no faster rate than the snail's pace—4/10 of 1 percent— which they maintain at present, the world would nonetheless be up to its current population of over 3 billion in 1970.

Population arithmetic like this is downright frightening! And that's just what it's supposed to be. It's supposed to frighten you, to panic you into doing something, now, to stop the population explosion. But, adhering to that old adage of *look before you leap,* prior to getting down to recommendations for population policy, let's take a more careful look at the not-so-simple arithmetic of population growth.

Forget about Luxembourg and Costa Rica for awhile, and take a look at population statistics for the United States. Ehrlich gives a doubling time of sixty-three years for the U.S., which translates into a per annum rate of about 1.1 percent. Does this mean that, unless we change our current patterns of reproductive behavior, by the 400th Fourth of July there will be 1.2 billion Americans saluting the flag and tossing beer cans into our lakes and rivers? It means no such thing. The key phrase is "our current patterns of reproductive behavior." What we must do is clarify the question of the relationship between our patterns of reproductive behavior and the rate of population growth.

We can begin by noticing that the much bandied-about Rate of Natural Increase is determined by a combination of two factors—our patterns of reproductive behavior and mortality *and* the age distribution of the population. If reproductive behavior were to remain unchanged over a great many years eventually a stable relationship between mortality-fertility patterns and the age distribution of the population would emerge, at which point the crude Natural Increase rate would accurately reflect long-term population trends. However, in periods when reproductive behavior has been changing in the recent past the Natural Increase figure may be very misleading. If the propensity to reproduce has fallen in the recent past, as it has in the U.S., the RNI exaggerates prospects for population growth. Why? Because people generally have children when they are young, and die when they are old. The people that are now in the high-mortality brackets are members of the relatively small generation born around the turn of the century, while those in the high fertility range are members of the much larger generation who were their children. If the currently fertile generation is having, on the

average, smaller families than their parents did, we may anticipate that
by the time they age, the numerical disproportion between generations
will be less than at present. This will automatically show up in higher
Crude Death Rates, lower Crude Birth Rates, and a lower Rate of Natural
Increase even if the average family size of children now being born does
not decrease further.

To avoid all this confusion and isolate the true, underlying trend
of population growth is a very complex mathematical problem. Without
getting too abstruse we can take one more step which may shed some
further light on the subject. Avoiding the terminology of birth and death
rates altogether, let us restate the conditions for population growth and
stability as follows: Take an imaginary group of female infants, all born
at the same moment. Follow them all through life until death, being
sure to count those who die in infancy. Count the total number of
female children born to members of this group in their 1000 lifespans.
Then take the ratio of daughters to mothers. This ratio is called the Net
Reproduction Rate (NRR). If the NRR is exactly equal to one, then the
population is just replacing itself. If it is less than one, the generation
of daughters has fewer members than the generation of mothers and the
population will shrink. If the NRR exceeds one, the population will
grow.

For the reasons given above, a fall in the NRR does not immediately show up in the rate of natural increase of population; yet it is
the NRR which is the crucial figure for long-run population growth.
Modern Japan provides a dramatic example. The CBR is 16.6 and the
CDR is 6.4, giving an RNI of 1.2 percent per annum. But does Japan
face a long-run population problem? Only if too few people are a
problem, for the underlying NRR of .92 tells us that after a few more
years of growth the Japanese population will, if current patterns prevail,
begin a long, steady decline!

What about the U.S.? The ponderous tomes in which professional
demographers advance their guarded estimates of trends in mortality,
fertility, and the Net Reproduction Rate are worth digging through.
From what I can gather, perusing this literature strictly as a layman, it
appears that the NRR in the U.S. has been falling for some time, is
already very close to the magic value of 1.0, and is expected to reach
that level and continue to drop below it sometime about 1975.[4]

This does not mean that the rate of population growth will im-

---

[4] See, for example, Donald J. Bogue, *Principles of Demography* (New York: John
Wiley & Sons, Inc., 1969), pp. 883–893.

mediately fall to zero in 1975. It may even accelerate slightly for a few years as the children of the postwar baby boom reach their age of maximum fertility. But soon, growth will taper off and finally population will gradually decline.

The likelihood that the NRR will soon fall below 1.0 has some interesting implications for some of the population control schemes advanced for this country. Consider an often mentioned scheme originated by the fertile imagination of Kenneth Boulding.[5] Boulding would require each mother to obtain a special permit or license before giving birth to a child. (Never mind how one would go about enforcing this against someone who showed up at the emergency room in labor without her ticket.) The permits would be distributed as follows: Each child, male and female, would be given one permit, good at any time, when they were born. Each married couple would thus automatically have two such permits. (If a child died in infancy its permit might revert to the parents to give them a second chance.) Any person, married or single, who did not want children could sell his permit to any couple who wanted a family of more than two.

Boulding evidently anticipates that a lively market would develop in these permits, rather like the Stock Exchange, with speculators, Dow-Jones indexes—the works. Many people have assumed that the price established for a certificate would be quite high, and have worried about such possibilities as rich whites buying up all the certificates of poor blacks. In fact, no such thing would happen. The price of a baby permit would clearly depend on the Net Reproduction Rate. As soon as the NRR fell to or below unity, as it appears about to do in this country, the price of certificates would automatically fall to zero! Any couple who wanted could have as many children as they pleased, despite the existence of this seemingly Draconian birth control legislation.

In my opinion, formed on the basis of what is currently known about demographic trends in the United States,[6] the best population policy for our government to adopt is no policy at all. Unfortunately, my opinion is not currently being heeded, for our government *does* now have some legislation on the books in this field. I am referring to the income tax exemption, and certain other government programs for

---

[5] In *The Meaning of the 20th Century* (New York: Harper & Row, 1964). An excerpt is included in the collection by Hardin, *op. cit.*
[6] Of course, if the unexpected were to happen, and the NRR to reverse its trend and rise abruptly, I might be willing to reopen this discussion.

child support, which encourage people to have large families. I can see no more justification for the government to subsidize population growth than to legislate against it. Family subsidies have to go. If the poor are to be given relief of some sort, let their payments be independent of family size. If programs like a guaranteed annual income are going to be instituted, make this income sufficient for a childless couple to live comfortably and a family of four to live decently. Any who would not avail themselves of the opportunities to keep their family size below eight or ten could justly be left either to scrimp and save and stretch their fixed guaranteed annual budget as best they could or to find, on their own initiative, some way of supplementing this budget. Cessation of all current government programs to promote population growth would, I should think, knock the last few points off the NRR even before 1975.

Is There an Optimal Population Size?

Perhaps some readers are convinced, by the argument advanced in the previous section, that population growth in the United States will one day soon spontaneously grind to a halt, but would still dispute the conclusion that no government population control measures are justified. For how do we know, these readers might say, that the level of population which we arrive at by chance will be the optimal level? Isn't it possible that population growth will stop too soon, leaving us with too few people? Or isn't it possible that population growth has already gone on too long, so that we are already overcrowded? Shouldn't we set some national goal of XYZ millions of persons, and make every effort to arrive at this goal in the shortest possible time?

Let us examine a few of the more frequently heard arguments on this score. A good starting point is the "Chamber of Commerce" argument, that large population size is good for business. If a sufficiently narrow conception of the phrase "good for business" is taken, there is some truth to the contention, for in comparing two communities of different size, or a single community at two periods in time, it is generally true that other things being equal the total volume of sales for all businesses will be larger when the community is more populous. But probing a little deeper, certain questions arise as to whether this fact, even if accepted as true, would justify an expansionary population policy. An expansion of the total sales for all businesses would not seem widely beneficial unless it represented at the same time an expansion of sales *per capita*. Suppose Smithville and Jonesville both start in 1960 with a population of 10,000 and total retail sales of $30 million ($3000 per capita). By 1970 Smithville doubles its population, and increases sales to $80 million ($4000 per capita), while Jonesville "stagnates," retaining its population of 10,000 and boosting its total volume of business to a mere $50 million ($5000 per capita). The Chamber of Commerce of Smithville will no doubt boast loud and long of the superior performance of their town, but where would you rather live? There is little basis in economic theory for the contention that increasing population makes business any better on a *per capita* basis.

Or is there? What about the more sophisticated variant of the "good for business" argument that says that population growth is necessary to keep us out of a recession? This turns out to be nothing but a rerun of the old "underconsumption" or "secular stagnation" argument. It is true that if a bungling government insisted on getting us into a permanent recession by pursuing deflationary monetary and fiscal policies year after year, a spurt of population growth *might* provide the spur for business recovery. But wouldn't it be better just to change economic policy? Proper management of fiscal and monetary policy could probably provide us with prosperity and rapid growth of per capita income even in a period of contracting population. Trying to use population control as an instrument of macroeconomic policy is about as enlightened a technique as burning down the barn to roast the pig.

Having dispatched the advocates of population control from the chambers of commerce, we must whirl about to face a new set of attackers, those from the Pentagon. These proponents of an expansionary population policy are bent on striking terror in our hearts with a formidable weapon indeed, a modernized, cyberneticized, cost-effectivized version of the "yellow peril"! As Colin Clark puts it, writing in the *National Review*,[7] "As far as we can see it now, the prospects for fifty years hence are of a world in which both the United States and Soviet Russia have fallen out of the race [for world power status] in a world dominated by the Asian countries, with India and China in the lead, and Pakistan and Indonesia as the runners up." For a moment (no longer), let us assume it is indeed true that the index of human well-being by which our government should be guided in its every decision is the maximizaton of military power at all costs. Must we then concede that population equals power? It is far from obvious that we must.

[7] May 20, 1969; reprinted in Walt Anderson, ed., *Politics and Environment* (Pacific Palisades, California: Goodyear Publishing Company, 1970).

Making war is like growing grain; you can do it with a lot of people with hoes or a few people with combines. And which is the more effective grain-growing force, the 300-million-man Indian "agricultural army" or the 20-million-man American force? Remember the Second World War? Those Germans put up an excellent fight against the combined forces of all the Allied countries, boasting many times the German population. The Allies won *not* by using a larger number of more poorly equipped troops. Quite the opposite, at first the Germans gained great victories with their initially more sophisticated equipment, and the tide was not turned until the Allies were able to overtake and surpass them in the output of military hardware.

I suspect that the inhabitants of "underpopulated" Sweden and the Netherlands, who lost their world-power status at the end of the 17th century, are laughing up their sleeves at American generals who would like to trade places with their Indian and Chinese counterparts. Come to think of it, if we exported all our generals to China, wouldn't that in itself be a partial solution to our population problem?

Next in line behind the generals as advocates of an activist population policy come assorted politicians and quasipolitical spokesmen. Among these a particularly interesting group of population growth advocates were flushed out by the results of the latest census. Every type of individual, it seems, has one overriding goal in life. For businessmen it is expansion of sales (or profits, if you take the old-fashioned view); for generals, it is augmentation of the kill capacity; and for mayors and governors, it appears to be the maximization of federal grants and subsidies. Now, since many of these federal grants and subsidies are handed out on a per capita basis, one way to get more money for your city is to get more·people into it. Never mind if per capita aid remains the same—it is the aggregate total which must grow to give you clout in the halls of Congress, and give you something to boast about at the next mayors' or governors' conference. So we saw the spectacle, when the census results were in, of outraged politicians everywhere crying that there must have been a miscount, that their fiefdom just *had* to have more inhabitants than the official tabulations showed.

But if the politicians who are *in* power want to increase the population, what about the politicians who are *out* of power? Naturally, they want more population too—at least if it is their own minority constituency where the multiplication takes place. This population-equals-power mentality is nowhere more evident than among those black leaders who cry "genocide" whenever education or legislation attempts to help our citizens freely choose the family size they would like. Their reasoning is that black people will, in the long run, be better off if they are more numerous, for then their voting power will increase. The last part is true enough, but will it be the black *people* or the black *politicians* who will be better off in this future era of stuffed ballot boxes and empty stomachs? It is interesting to note in passing that the "genocide" line is popular even among those radicals who admit the futility of advancing welfare via the ballot box, for they are interested in a maximum supply of cannon fodder to man the barricades on the day of the revolution. (I would not wish to imply that blacks as an ethnic group have a monopoly on any of the above lines of reasoning.)

All of the special interest groups mentioned so far have had one thing in common: Their idea of the optimal population is larger than the numbers we have at present. The conservationists, in contrast, want a population smaller than the current one. They have their own interests to defend. Just as generals want recruits, and politicians want huddled masses yearning to pay taxes and collect subsidies, conservationists have a burning desire for wide-open spaces and wilderness areas— trampled and crowded by the minimum possible number of fellow backpackers and naturalists. Since nature lovers seem to be born in a certain fixed proportion to the population, and since the prospects for further expansion of wilderness areas are, to say the least, dim, it follows with logical precision that the smaller the population the better off will be those conservationists among them.

But conservationists will say, "You are making a parody of us! We are not like those other special interest groups—the militarists, the politicians, or the greedy Capitalists! We speak for the interests of society as a whole, and have sound, reasoned arguments to back up our position." Fair enough. Let's take a look at these arguments.

A full-page ad in *The New York Times* [8] maintains that the fight against pollution "will be a losing battle unless we check our rapidly growing population, which is an underlying cause of the pollution of our environment." This doctrine, I submit, is at best highly misleading and at worst utterly fallacious. It is simply not true *either* that population growth necessarily causes increased pollution of the environment *or* that a halt to population growth would by itself stabilize or decrease the

[8] September 27, 1970, Section E., p. 7.

amount of pollution produced by our economy. The two problems of population pressure and pollution abatement are, both conceptually and in practice, quite separate and distinct.

Harking back to what was said on the subject in an earlier chapter, it will be recalled that an act of pollution is a form of trespass on the rights or property of others, an act in which individual A imposes a cost or burden on individual B without providing any compensation to the victim. A variety of antipollution measures was proposed to deal with various forms of environmental abuse commonly encountered, each of which was designed to have the effect of making the would-be polluter bear the entire cost of whatever production or consumption activity he chose to engage in. Enactment and universal enforcement of a comprehensive set of such measures would make it unprofitable to commit any pollution trespass, and if any such act were committed by accident the injured party would have the right to full compensation. The effectiveness of none of these pollution control measures in any way depends on the population density of the region within which they are enforced. It is true that *without pollution control*, more population means more pollution. But a highway traveled by 1 million smog-free electric cars does not produce any more smog than a highway traveled by one such car; the total amount of smog produced is zero in each case. If you want to control pollution, go at it directly, not via the back-door measure of population control.

Even if we were so clumsy as to try to control pollution by stopping population growth (Remember burning down the barn to roast the pig?) we would fail in our objective. Conservationists who advocate this approach are guilty of one of the same fallacies as the chambers of commerce mentioned above, namely, that the *economy* will stop growing if *population* stops growing. In the opening paragraph of their book Rienow and Rienow write:

> Every 8 seconds a new American is born. He is a disarming little thing, but he begins to scream loudly in a voice that can be heard for seventy years. He is screaming for 56,000,000 gallons of water, 21,000 gallons of gasoline, 10,150 pounds of meat, 28,000 pounds of milk and cream, 9,000 pounds of wheat, and great storehouses of all other foods, drinks, and tobaccos. These are his lifetime demands on the economy.[9]

Their implication is that if this child were not born, the 21,000

---

[9] *Moment in the Sun*, p. 3.

gallons of gasoline and other demands, plus all the concomitant refuse and pollution would never need to be produced. This is false, for the economy would keep right on growing without him. Most of the 21,000 gallons of gasoline would still be produced, but would not go to this child. Instead they would be split up in such a way as to increase the per capita gasoline consumption of the remaining population. As long as strong pollution control measures are not instituted to raise the ratio of Type I to Type II GNP (see Chapter 1), our environment will just get dirtier and dirtier as time goes on, whether population growth stops or not.

This population-pollution fallacy is not the only conservationist argument for population control. A second is based on the phenomenon of pure crowding, external effects aside. Reducing this argument to its barest essentials, suppose two young married couples, the Campbells and the Schwartzes, are shipwrecked on a small, but quite habitable island in the middle of nowhere. Each couple looks forward with pleasure to the prospect of producing sons and daughters to perpetuate themselves, but in doing so, it is clear that a possible conflict between two factors exists. On the one hand, the total parental satisfaction of each couple would be greater, the greater the number of offspring in the family. On the other, their parental satisfaction per child, if you can conceive of measuring such a thing, will be less the less comfortable the conditions in which these children will have to live out their lives. Suppose the Campbells say to themselves, if the Schwartzes are going to have a large family the island will get pretty crowded, but if that's the way it's going to be, then we'd rather have four kids growing up on a crowded island than one or two kids growing up on a crowded island. If the Schwartzes reason the same way chances are the island will rapidly reach the level of overpopulation which we defined earlier as the "marginal subsistence solution."

Isn't this really foolish behavior for the islanders? Wouldn't they be better off getting together and making an agreement that each would have two children only, on the grounds that to have two children grow up to live a prosperous life is better than to have four grow up to live a life of strife and starvation? If such an agreement is beneficial for the islanders, doesn't the same reasoning apply to all the people of the United States? Wouldn't we all be better off sacrificing the small freedom of having a large family in return for the great benefit of having our small families grow up in an uncrowded environment?

It must be admitted that this line of reasoning does display a certain sophistication and theoretical elegance which surpasses anything we have encountered so far. In fact, it amounts to an entirely different approach to the question of the optimal population size. Instead of the absurdity of trying to find a single numerical value for population which would somehow be best for everyone, and which would then become the goal of government population policy, this line of reasoning attempts to justify collective action on behalf of population control by establishing that the invisible hand does not provide us with an *efficient* solution to the population size problem. And, as was demonstrated with the simplified example of the islanders, it is possible to imagine situations in which collectively agreeing upon some set of decisions concerning family size, other than those which would be made freely and independently, might be mutually beneficial to all members of the community.

The principal difficulty with this as a guide to practical population policy is that it is a sword which cuts both ways. Just put the Campbells and the Schwartzes on a very large island. Now the Campbells might reason as follows: "Each child which we raise will be an added expense for us, so we are reluctant to have more than a few. But we would like to see these children grow up in a community of sufficient size to provide a varied social life, the possibility for specialization in the division of labor, and the opportunity for cooperation in defense against jungle beasts. Therefore, let us propose an agreement with the Schwartzes that if they will have a few extra children to act as companions, mates, and helpers of ours, then we, in return, will bear the added expense of a few more children of our own." Returning from the island to the U.S., couldn't we find people saying, "Let us tax small families and subsidize large ones, each of us giving up the small amount of freedom implied in order that our children can grow up in a world where retail sales are stronger, and our country is a leading military power!"

If the free-rider problem could be overcome, all the small-population advocates might conceivably agree mutually to restrict family size, and all the big-population advocates might agree mutually to expand family size. It is then rather difficult to see exactly what the outcome would be in a community where these two parties were anywhere near equal in numbers. Could an efficient, mutually beneficial arrangement be negotiated between the two groups? Perhaps members of each might band together and offer subsidies to members of the other to reverse their allegiance. This attempt would probably fail because some individuals would try to cheat, feigning the opposite of their true opinion in order to collect the subsidy from their fellows. It is difficult to believe that the hypothetically possible efficient move to a strictly voluntary collective population policy could ever be arranged in practice in a large community of widely divergent opinions.

We are left in a rather unsatisfactory position. We cannot hope to find a magic number optimal population target; yet we cannot rigorously establish that the population which results from free and individual decisions represents a state of efficiency, let alone of global optimality. It seems that we are left with the choice either of permitting one sub-group of the population to impose its favored population policy on the rest, against their will via the political process, or of pursuing a completely laissez-faire population policy despite the theoretical difficulties which this will encounter. In practice, I favor the laissez-faire approach, for two sound reasons. First, the *burden of proof* must always rest with the proponents of any positive action by the state which involves the restriction of the freedom of individuals, whether allegedly for their own good or not, and this burden of proof cannot now be met by the advocates either of population expansion or reduction. Second, it appears that if current demographic trends in the United States are left to work themselves out spontaneously, we will have a population with as reasonable characteristics of size and stability as any population target likely to be hammered out via the devious channels of democratic choice and legislative compromise.

chapter 6

ENVIRONMENTAL PROBLEMS AND ECONOMIC DEVELOPMENT

Even the idea of attempting to discuss the subject of economic development in one small chapter must seem ludicrous to any reader who has seen the long shelves of books on the topic housed in the average university library stacks. Anyone familiar with the content and not just the number of such books will doubtless be more skeptical still, for the notorious tendency of economists to be unable to agree on a single matter of theory or policy is even more pronounced among development specialists than in the rest of the profession. Nonetheless the attempt must be made, for those long, subtle chains of cause and effect upon which the science of ecological economics focuses its attention have a disturbing way of sneaking across national frontiers and across the boundaries that separate the "developed" from the "underdeveloped" world.

In order to keep from drifting too far way from our main topic this chapter will be limited to a consideration of the ways in which specifically *environmental* aspects of the development problem relate to the conduct of American policy toward developing countries. Within these self-imposed limits, the two most important problem areas concern world trade in natural resources and the population explosion in the underdeveloped world.

Are We Exploiting the Third World?

One of the statistical tidbits frequently encountered in the numerous popular books available on the environmental crisis is that the United States, with some 6 percent of the world's population, consumes a vastly greater percentage than this of the world's raw materials. Figures for individual products can be calculated with a fair degree of accuracy, for example, a fourth of all the world's potash (and beer), a third of all tin, half of all newsprint. Aggregate statistics are a good deal less reliable, but range from 30 to 50 percent of *all* the world's nonrenewable natural resources of *all* kinds. A great and increasing fraction of this total is imported from developing countries. The U.S. imports virtually all of its chrome, cobalt, manganese, nickel, and tin; about half of its lead, tungsten, and zinc; and increasingly large quantities of products of which it has long been considered a leading producer, such as oil, iron ore, and copper.

Could it be that we are taking more than our fair share of these things? Do the statistics on the flow of natural resources from the underdeveloped to the developed world imply an exploitation of the former by the latter? What do we mean by "exploitation" anyway? Are we appropriating resources without giving just compensation? Does our resource consumption pattern hinder the development of third world trading partners?

Before leaping to any conclusions in answer to these questions the reader would be well-advised to pause and apply his now extensive knowledge of economic theory to the matter of trade between nations. He will discover that the simple fact of our large primary product imports does not, standing by itself, indicate that anyone is being exploited. At first glance the exact opposite might more likely be indicated.

What we call trade is nothing more than the common organizational means used to extract the potential for mutual benefit from a situation of economic inefficiency. It would be inefficient for the butcher to have all those hundreds of pounds of meat and for me to have none, so we trade, and both profit thereby. If either he or I were to propose an exchange on the basis of *terms of trade* which were *not* mutually beneficial, I would choose to become a vegetarian or he would choose to retain excess inventories rather than engage in a transaction that left either of us less well off than before. Juxtaposition of the terms "exploitation" and "free trade" represents self-contradiction.

Mutual gains are as much a natural result of trade between the United States and the developing world as between the butcher and me. The gains to the U.S. are obvious. Our huge industrial machine and astronomical (by world historical measures) standard of living gobble up huge doses of materials which we either cannot produce, or cannot produce cheaply, at home. Without them, our output and consumption could not be maintained at the present levels with current technology.

The advantage gained from trade by the developing country is usually thought of in terms of an opportunity for accelerated economic growth rather than simply for increased current consumption (although the latter would also be possible). Let us consider a country rich in oil. Even without world trade a country with good oil resources would have a distinct advantage in development, being able to use the product in many ways as a lubricant, a fuel, and the source of a huge variety of synthetic materials, even synthetic food. At first the amount of oil used would be small, for the equipment to extract it, refine it, transport it, and be lubricated and fueled by it would have to be painstakingly accumulated step by step on the basis of the primitive industrial establishment and limited investment potential of the home country. Trade offers an obvious shortcut to development. An oil-hungry developed nation, already having depleted its own supplies, might be willing to trade sophisticated industrial plant and equipment for the oil which the underdeveloped country could not use in any event until the distant future.

The oil producing country is faced with a clear choice: It can leave future generations struggling to pull themselves up by their own bootstraps atop a sea of petroleum reserves, or it can present these same future citizens with a modernized, prosperous economy, running low on oil but equipped with the technological and industrial flexibility to diversify its energy base to suit these conditions. If the latter path is chosen, members of those future generations will thank today's decision makers for permitting the greedy trading partner to swallow up far more than its share of the world oil reserves, for look what they got in return!

Despite the logical appeal of this line of argument, and despite the existence of many instances in which things have worked out more-or-less along these lines, we cannot leave the matter here. For although it may be true that developing nations can *potentially* benefit from the export of their natural resources to industrialized regions, for a variety of reasons they do not always succeed in realizing their end of the potential mutual gains from trade. Let us see why this is so.

First, it happens that export of raw materials is a shortcut to development *only* under the condition that export earnings are wisely and productively invested in development activities. But if underdeveloped countries were equipped with efficient governments, thrifty propertied classes, and armies of dynamic indigenous entrepreneurs, they would not still be underdeveloped today! The literature on development economics is jampacked with horror stories of lavish presidential palaces, rows of diplomats' Mercedes, fat numbered Swiss bank accounts, jet planes and submarines bought as playthings to pay off soldier-politicians—all purchased out of earnings from the export of the nation's irreplaceable patrimony of natural resources. Small wonder the term "kleptocracy" has been coined to describe the political system of these unfortunate lands where the government gets gaudier and gaudier as the nation gets poorer and poorer. More sobering still is the fact that even honest and prudent governments, in the countries lucky enough to have them, are not always able to avoid errors, misconceptions, and blind alleys in development planning which also waste many hard-earned resources.

If the people of the developing nations are being exploited by their own domestic regimes, it might be maintained that the alleged imperialist powers which trade with them are not at fault and that the victims have only themselves to blame if they do not throw the rascals out. This might be a telling argument, were it not for the realities of cold war politics. All too often honest and capable leaders are left to languish while Moscow and Washington lavish diplomatic, military, and economic support of their corrupt client dictatorships and plot to oust one another's kleptocratic puppets. The third world might well be hindered in its development by this kind of "trade."

Second, the doctrine that world commerce in primary products is beneficial to both the developed and developing partners is robbed of much of its force unless that trade is genuinely free trade. Unfortunately, free trade is a principle all too often honored in the breach. The very fact that trade so frequently takes the form of sales and negotiations between *governments,* rather than directly between individual citizens of different countries, is a clear indication of this fact. Even trade among governments is not free, but encumbered by an incredible network of tariffs, quotas, split exchange rates, tie-in sales, taxes, subsidies, restrictions, and regulations. It is often charged, and not easy to disprove, that the domination of the world trade and monetary systems by a handful of industrial powers is used to keep raw material prices low and sources of supply open.

We have not yet mentioned the grossest violation of free trade —the immigration restrictions (and in certain well-known cases, emigration restrictions as well) enforced by virtually every state on the surface of the globe. How can the governments of rich countries claim to have the interests of the poor of the underdeveloped world at heart if they insist on preventing their own employers from offering work to the unemployed of other nations? I think any American who speaks altruistically of stepping up our foreign aid, and at the same time grows rich behind our severe immigration barriers, deserves a nomination for hypocrite of the month.

Finally, an element of truth may be discovered in the arguments of those who charge neocolonial exploitation, if we stop to consider the "advantages of coming second" in comparison to "the advantages of coming first." Second comers, we are often told, have the tremendous developmental advantage of being able to borrow from the technology of those who came first. (Just think what a great advantage it would have been for the U.S., Britain, or Germany if a little green man in a flying saucer touched down in the year 1790 or so, and had patiently explained the Bessemer process for making steel!) Yet the advantages of developing in a world full of advanced technology could be offset for latecomers by a matching disadvantage—that of growing up in a world where all those export earnings and all that wizard technology had to be harnessed to synthesizing once-abundant natural products and to processing abysmally low-grade ores at astronomical expense.

Imagine that the munificent beneficence of international capitalism has provided the oil-exporting nation of our previous example with a huge, modern refinery, all paid for out of royalties and export earnings. When the last oil has been pumped up from beneath the sands will a "fourth world" suddenly appear from which this country can import *its* raw materials? Or will the refinery be left as a huge rusting white elephant in the desert, while its highly trained but narrowly specialized labor force goes back to herding camels?

Ultimately, a study of the dismal science of ecological economics leads one to the conclusion that the second-comers had best begin thinking of some alternative future for themselves other than economic "development" as defined by the example of the first-comers. Development in the past has simply meant growth of Type II GNP, but the prospects for bringing the entire world up to the present American level of industrialization on the basis of a throughput technology are virtually nil. There just are not enough sources and sinks in the world to do it. Sooner or later both developed and underdeveloped countries will be forced to make the transition to an ecologically viable economy.[1] There can be no doubt that learning to live within the limits of one's environment will be a harder task for the poor than for the rich to face.

To summarize, although the simple belief that a nation is being exploited unless it is allowed to keep all of its manganese ore for domestic consumption appears to be a serious oversimplification, it must be admitted that the policies, and sometimes simply the existence, of industrialized countries often make life more difficult than it need be for the second-comers. Whether the label of "imperialist exploitation" is or is not applied to what has gone on in the past is relatively unimportant. The important task for development economics now is to begin thinking about the future and how the third world can learn to cope with problems of population, resources, and environment from which we Americans miraculously escaped in the course of our own growth from poverty to prosperity.

Population, Loaves, and Fishes

In the last chapter we came to the guardedly optimistic conclusion that the population of the United States may be expected in time to

[1] Chapter 8 of this book contains a discussion of what such an economy might look like.

evel off at a figure which would permit a standard of living well above
he subsistence level.[2]

The question now is whether a similar optimism is justified with
espect to the demographic situation in developing countries. The
nswer is *no*. The crucial difference lies in a relationship between
opulation growth and the level of development called the *demographic
ransition*.

The phenomenon of the demographic transition can be easily
nderstood by looking at Figure 6.1. Section A shows how birth and
eath rates respond to the process of economic development. At a very
ow level of development both birth and death rates are high. As the
rocess of development begins, increasing prosperity makes better nutri-
on and medical care available. This brings about a drop in the death
ate. Economic development also affects the birth rate, but not in such
 simple and rapid fashion. It takes considerable time for the complex
ffects of cultural change, the spread of literacy and education, increas-
g urbanization, and other factors to have any impact on the birth
ate. Eventually, as the transition to a modern industrialized, urbanized
ociety is completed, the birth rate falls, narrowing the gap between
irths and deaths once again.

Part of the figure shows what happens to the rate of population
rowth during the process of demographic transition. Since, as will be
ecalled, the rate of population growth at a given moment is calculated
s the difference between the Crude Birth Rate and Crude Death Rate,
opulation growth is low *both* at very low and very high levels of de-
elopment. During the transitional phase, when "death control" has
aken effect and birth control has not, population grows explosively.
s a result the curve relating population growth to economic develop-
ent has a distinct hump in the middle.

It is this hump which is the primary cause of pessimism concern-
g the population problem in developing countries. It would be nice
 we could be sure that in time the natural course of events would

Certain assumptions were necessary to support this, and violation of any one
f them might upset the conclusion. It was necessary to assume that current
ends in reproductive behavior would not sharply reverse themselves; that the
overnment would have the wisdom to abstain from active promotion of popu-
tion growth; and that the programs for pollution abatement, wilderness preser-
ation, and so on set forth in other sections of this book would be implemented;
nce without these it is difficult for our environment to contain even our
resent population comfortably.

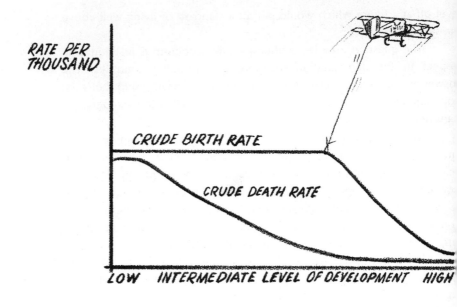

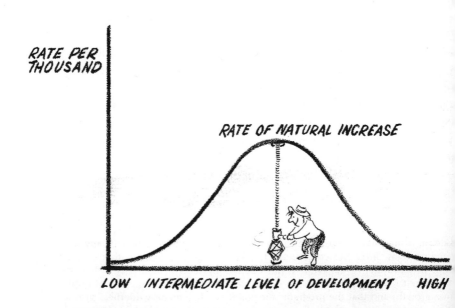

FIGURE 6.1 The demographic transition

carry these nations through, as happened in the past to all of today's already developed nations. Unfortunately, getting over the hump may be more difficult in the future than it was in the past.

For one thing the hump is higher than it used to be. America and Western Europe underwent the demographic transition in the last century in a period when medical technology was in a very primitive state as compared to today. Thus the death rate curve fell neither so soon, so sharply, nor so far as in the 20th century when Western medicine has been imported wholesale into the third world, sometimes cutting the death rate by more than half in a single decade.

Today's higher hump raises the ominous possibility that countries caught to the left of it may get stuck in a "population trap" and never make it over at all. This could happen because rising population growth lowers the rate of growth of per capita income, even while the growth rate of GNP in absolute terms continues at a constant rate. If population growth catches up to the rate of growth of GNP, "development" in any meaningful sense ceases and poverty is simply reproduced on larger and larger scale each year.

In addition to the danger of the population trap, developing countries today face the prospect that time is simply running out for them. The developed nations could afford a hundred years or more to work their way at a leisurely pace through the demographic transition. In those days a new continent was being opened, and a seemingly limitless abundance of sources and sinks permitted "quick and dirty" throughput methods of industrialization. Neither time, space, nor resources will permit a repetition of this process on a world-wide scale now.

Given this difficult situation, what policy alternatives are available to us and to the leaders of the developing nations themselves? The available alternatives were succinctly expressed more than a century ago by John Stuart Mill:

> Society can feed the necessitous if it takes their multiplication under control, or (if destitute of all moral feeling for the wretched offspring) it can leave the last to their discretion, abandoning the first to their own care. But it cannot with impunity take the feeding upon itself, and leave the multiplying free.[3]

J. S. Mill, *Principles of Political Economy* (New York: Appleton, Century, Crofts, 1881), p. 447. Cited in John M. Culbertson, *Economic Development, An Ecological Approach* (New York: Alfred A. Knopf, 1971), Chapter 4.

Many observers of world population and development today seem to be suffering from a sort of "omnipotence complex" which prevents them from making a reasoned choice among Mill's three alternatives. Just as many Pentagon strategists suffer from the delusion that there is no limit to what American military power can accomplish by way of influencing the course of world politics, these people think that there is no limit to the ability of American industry, agriculture, and technology to shape the course of world economic development. Observing the tendency of world population to grow at geometric rates, they leap to the conclusion that we "must" somehow feed all those additional people who are on their way into the world; and from there, they leap to the still more fantastic conclusion that we not only "must" but *can* do this.

In effect, these people are proposing that we plunge ahead into the third alternative, hoping for some sort of miracle of loaves and fishes to save us from the consequences. As Mill clearly foresaw, in warning against this policy, the only effect of pursuing it would be to activate the "utterly dismal theorem," and to insure that world population would in the end reach the absolute subsistence, rather than the marginal subsistence, level with everyone reduced to a common denominator of misery.

Many other would-be policy advisers, seeing the folly of pursuing this third alternative, opt for the first instead. They advocate undertaking the task of feeding those who cannot feed themselves, but, recognizing that loaves and fishes are available only in finite quantities, advocate taking "multiplication" under control at the same time. With this approach they hope to avoid both the marginal and absolute subsistence equilibria, hastening the world to the prosperous zone of population stability lying to the right of the population hump.

Examination of current and past programs undertaken to curb population growth in developing countries leads one to conclude that these people too must be suffering from an omnipotence complex. The idea that an army of American peace corpsmen, armed with shiploads of IUD's and contraceptive pills, can change the reproductive habits of two-thirds of the world's population overnight is about as realistic as it was to think that 100,000 U.S. Marines would be able to win a quick and decisive military victory in Vietnam. I do not want to belittle totally the importance of such efforts at birth control as have been undertaken, but merely to emphasize that their actual impact has been very small so far in comparison to the magnitude of the global problem, and that at best their effects on population growth are felt only over a long period.

To predict that we will be unable to accomplish miracles does not preclude a discussion of how the limited amount of aid which will presumably be forthcoming from developed countries might best be put to use. It is an important principle of economics that the less of something there is, the more care must be taken in allocating it. In this connection one of the most sensible suggestions which I have run across is that made by William and Paul Paddock, who advocate using the principle of "tirage" to allocate future aid to developing nations.[4] Battlefield doctors, following the tirage principle, refuse to treat either those who are in pain but will survive without treatment, or those who will die no matter what treatment they receive. Instead, they concentrate their limited facilities exclusively on those who would respond to care but would die without. By analogy, the Paddocks recommend concentrating all aid on those marginal countries which might just be able to make it over the hump, but only with outside help. They reason that it is wasteful to devote any aid to those who are already on the downhill run, even though they will suffer certain hardships before completing their development. It is equally wasteful to help those who would not be able to escape the population trap despite our maximum efforts. By helping only the middle group, at least we can hope that our attempts to do good will actually do at least some good.

Yet what will become of those nations written off as hopeless? I suppose that there is some possibility of undue pessimism, and that the "green revolution" will succeed in carrying even these nations through the demographic transition without excessive difficulties. (Still, I cannot see that any harm will be done by preparing for the worst now.)

More likely, the latter part of this century will witness some instances of the massive riots, plagues, and famines foreseen by the prophets of doom. If such events do come to pass, it is at least possible that they will cure, by a sort of cruel shock treatment, the problems which the cold war competition in foreign aid cannot hope to resolve. In the end the abrupt rise in death rates and disorder predicted by the pessimists may ironically turn out to be the instrument for achieving the hope of the optimists, namely, an acceleration of social and cultural

[4] See *Famine 1975!* (Boston: Little, Brown & Company, 1967).

change resulting in a declining birth rate and a rude completion of the demographic transition.

Perhaps the reader will be disappointed by my suggestion that there is little or nothing we can do about the population explosion in underdeveloped countries. The sad fact is that we live in a world in which some problems exist which simply do not have tidy solutions waiting to be discovered by the inquiring mind of man. Given the realities of the situation, I think that the best we can do is to avoid being misguided by false hopes into undertaking policies which will do more harm than good.

True, widely held precepts of morality demand that we heal the sick and feed the hungry, but can we do this if the only result will be to increase the number of sick and hungry to be cared for in the next round? As one writer put it, "If ethical principles deny our right to do evil in order that good may come, are we justified in doing good when the forseeable consequence is evil?" [5]

[5] A. V. Hill, in Hardin, *op. cit.*, p. 78.

chapter 7

PRESERVING THE WILDERNESS—
PUBLIC INTEREST OR SPECIAL INTEREST?

On Good Economics and Good Government

In Chapter 4 it was argued that the use of general tax revenue to finance projects offering special benefits to a fraction of the population is both bad economics and bad government. It is bad economics since, except in the limiting case where all political decisions are made under the rule of unanimity, each such project will generally be funded beyond the point where the marginal cost of the project equals its marginal benefit. The necessary conditions for efficiency are violated and misallocation of resources results. The use of public funds for such projects is also bad government, because the nonbeneficiary taxpayers are forced to invest a part of their earnings in a way which at best yields them no returns and, more often, causes them positive harm.

Get any good conservationist into a discussion on the subject of the Army Corps of Engineers or the Department of Highways and you will find an ardent supporter of this idea. He will curse the incredible waste and corruption involved in the history of massive federal give-aways to lumbering, mining, grazing, hydroelectric, and construction interests, and then curse them again because he as a taxpayer has been forced not only to suffer from the results of these criminal actions but actually to finance his own suffering!

If you really want to see some fireworks, ask this same conservationist if these same principles of government and economics apply to such projects as national parks and wilderness preservation programs. Ask him why it is that if justice requires motorists to pay for their own roads, hydroelectric firms to pay for their own dams, golfers to pay for their own golf courses, and gourmets to pay for their own escargots, lovers of the wilderness should not pay for their own wilderness and campers for their own campsites? Why should the special interests of conservationists be subsidized by the taxes of nonconservationists?

You would be well-advised to wear a verbal flak vest while asking this question, because your conservationist interlocutor is armed with quite an arsenal of replies. Let's devote a few pages to an examination of these replies.

I, too, am a wilderness lover, a member of the beneficiary group of conservation legislation, and you may be sure that I have asked these hard questions of myself a good many times and that I am really going to make sure that we sift these replies for any possible shred of a valid argument. I will also suggest some guidelines for a much more effective wilderness preservation program than the National Park system, one which is within the bounds of both good economics and good government.

Conservation and the Public Interest

The first gambit of the conservationist in defending public financing of his favorite projects is to argue that conservation and wilderness preservation is not a special interest at all, but, instead, the common interest of the whole population. This contention is without basis in fact. In the absence of strong evidence to the contrary, it seems safe to assume that

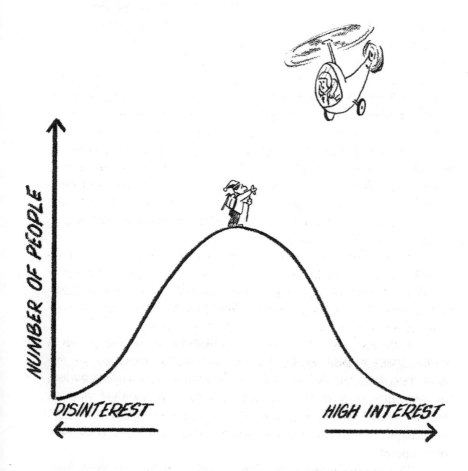

FIGURE 7.1 Hypothetical distribution of the population with respect to their interest in wilderness preservation

the distribution of the populace with respect to their degree of interest in wilderness preservation looks something like the curve shown in Figure 7.1. The horizontal scale represents the degree of an individual's interest in wilderness preservation. Toward the right are located the real hard core enthusiasts. These include the 12,000 rugged devotees who visited Rainbow Bridge in the first fifty years after its discovery, making the difficult trip up or down river or twenty-eight miles overland by horseback. Somewhat to the left of them come the average backpacker whom one meets along sections of trail more, let us say, than five miles from the nearest road. Further toward the middle are the hundreds of thousands who make a visit to some of our more developed and accessible parks for a weekend or two out of the year, those who appreciate the wilderness through the window of a car, or who are content to patronize a modest state park near their home. At the extreme left of the scale are those who not only get no benefit from the wilderness but view it with positive displeasure, those who look at a tree and think what a waste that it has not yet been turned into a lovely residence or a page of their favorite magazine.

I will make no pretense at putting numbers on the vertical scale or dollar values along the horizontal, but we may be certain that this is a reality: a *few* people who benefit enormously from our national parks, a *great many* who derive a moderate benefit, and a *few* who are positively upset at the thought of a tree looking at a tree.

If the tax burden is assumed to be distributed over the members of this group without respect for the position of individuals on the scale, then it is clear that for any given wilderness preservation project the individual share of the costs will outweigh the individual share of the benefits for all those to the left of a certain point. Government financing of such a project serves only the interests of those to the right of this point.

The conservationists are hardly willing to give up their fight simply because the benefits of the projects which they propose are not distributed with exact mathematical equality among the entire population. Even conceding *this* point, they are able to return to the attack with a number of other reasons for including wilderness preservation among the items receiving government subsidies.

One of the most frequently heard of these is the argument from irreversibility. Suppose, it is said, that you cut down a stand of virgin redwood forest to make lumber, or dam a beautiful canyon to generate electricity. In a few years the housing may have less value than you thought, or atomic power may make the dam obsolete, but no matter how much you regret your decision the trees or canyon are gone forever. But if you mistakenly reserve an area for a park and if, in a few years, you find that interest in this particular park is less than you had thought, or if a really pressing need for timber or power develops, you can easily reverse your decision. Therefore, the argument goes, if there is any doubt in the marginal cases of commercial development versus wilderness preservation, it is best to play safe and decide in favor of the latter.

I think the irreversibility argument contains a grain of truth, but that as an argument for government spending on wilderness preservation its importance has been greatly exaggerated. It is simply not true that the destruction of wilderness areas is irreversible, except in the narrow case where the value of an area lies in its virginity per se. Pure virgin wilderness, although important and extremely valuable, is only a part of the total land available for recreational use.

To anyone who has been to Vermont during the October foliage season or visited the Smoky Mountains, an area which is in much better condition today than when it first became a park, certain Western conservationists, with their haughty contempt for second-growth woodland, must seem a bit narrowminded.

Many conservationists are extremely suspicious of the concept of wilderness restoration because the idea has often been misused in support of the erroneous contention that our remaining virgin areas need not be handled with care. But by refusing even to consider restoration where it is possible, I think they are doing themselves a disservice in the long run.

For those areas like the largest virgin redwoods and sequoias, where restoration is impossible, there is some validity to the irreversibility argument. Consider Figure 7.2. This little graph shows the value, for each year in the 20th century, of a certain site in its alternative uses as a park and for commercial exploitation. To read the graph for any year you measure the commercial value down from the top straight line to the wavy line; and to measure its value as a park you read up from the bottom. The dashed line in the middle shows the breakeven point. The figure has a wedge shape because, as population and GNP grow, the value of the site in both alternative uses increases. As you can see, although there are some year-to-year fluctuations, the wavy line stays

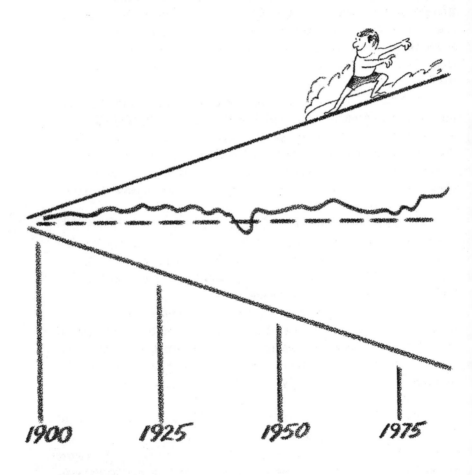

FIGURE 7.2 Best land use over time

above the breakeven point most of the time, indicating that the best use of the land is as a park, despite the fact that for a few years during the Second World War its current commercial value momentarily exceeded its recreational value. If this land had been logged over or flooded in those years and lost forever to recreation, would this have been a wise use of resources? Without going into technical details, it is possible that because of lack of foresight or temporary emergency conditions this particular wilderness area might have been destroyed and thus lost forever to its best use.[1]

Stated in this form, the irreversibility argument does not indicate that federal ownership and control of our national parks is a necessity for shielding the legitimate interests of conservationists from irreversible damage caused by wars, abnormally high interest rates, or other temporary crises. To the extent that the argument is valid, it does argue for a maximum of procedural barriers and delays to be placed in the way of transferring certain sites from recreational to commercial use. The worst situation would be the one which now prevails for vast tracts of the most valuable federal land where some administrator, at the stroke of a pen, can at any moment make the irreversible decision in question. Conservationists have realized this, and have lobbied for legislation like the Wilderness Bill, which in effect requires that the stroke of the pen be made by Congress, not an administrative agency. This clearly is a help, since as we all know, Congressional decision making is slow and replete with procedural delays. But Congressional decision making is also subject to strong pressures from commercial interests, and in time of war from military interests as well. Wouldn't it be safer if the *conservationists themselves* had control over these irreversible decisions, rather than relying on the whim of a bureaucrat or the treachery of a politician? If, let us say, the Sierra Club *owned* the site in question, they would sell it to be logged only if they were pretty sure that the decision

[1] Those readers with a background in business or economics will recognize that the ability of the market to insure the best use of resources in cases like this one depends on the ability of capital markets to smooth out irregular fluctuations in the curve of Figure 7.2 by discounting future values at the prevailing rate of interest. If interest rates always accurately reflected the underlying preferences of individuals concerning present versus future benefits, then the irreversibility argument would lose its validity altogether. But if, as is the case in the real world, capital markets are subject to controls and imperfections, and if the rate of interest reflects not the preferences of the community but merely the momentary and perhaps misguided policies of the Federal Reserve Board, it is possible that irreversible mistakes might be made.

was a wise one, only if, for example, the price were high enough to purchase or improve a superior site elsewhere. If conservationists *really* wanted to lock this site into use as a park, they could not only buy it but write a covenant into the deed which would prevent its sale for commercial use even by future administrators of the Club itself.

In sum, the irreversibility argument turns out to work not in favor of extending our national park system as it now exists but of turning it into a system of private parks to provide surer protection for the future!

As soon as the subject of selling the national parks to the Sierra Club is raised, conservationists come up with another set of arguments in favor of government action, which I will call the organizational arguments. Commercial interests, it is said, are concentrated and well-organized, while conservation interests are badly organized and diffuse. Thus, commercial interests would be able to raise the money to outbid the conservationists, even if the latter might actually be able to make better use of the land. This argument can take several forms. Let's see what truth there is in any of them.

It is sometimes alleged that there is a free rider problem with the national parks. This arises not because a few irresponsible recreationists might sneak past the turnstile at the entrance to the park, using it without paying, but because the parks provide benefits, in the form of externalities or spillover effects, to those who never visit them. National parks should be considered as a public good, albeit an imperfect one, which like education provides major values to the direct beneficiary, but also furnishes significant external benefits to others in society.

Is this all so? Do you get any external benefits from Yosemite National Park, which you have never visited and which, for purposes of the argument, let's say you never will? If so, just what are these benefits?

For a start we might try to measure the extent of these benefits by the strength of the sense of outrage which you would feel if you read one morning that the park had been converted into a test range for new defoliants for use in Vietnam. That might cause you sufficient pain to mail a check to the Save Yosemite Committee, but you also might not bother, hoping that others would do so and make you a free rider. Perhaps the externality takes the form of the increased range of choice among parks, even though you don't choose to visit Yosemite itself. Or perhaps it is that you can benefit from pictures which Ansel Adams takes there, although you may never see the place with your own eyes. Or perhaps the parks which you do use are less crowded and the entrance fees are lower because Yosemite takes the pressure off.

This is an impressive list. It must be admitted by even the most skeptical that we would be less well off were Yosemite to be despoiled. But does this list of "external effects" justify subsidizing the national park system? If it does, I submit, then subsidy of almost any good or service imaginable would also be so justified, since effects like the above are present almost everywhere in the economy.

Let's look at automobiles, for example. When, a few years ago, a change in federal safety standards took the old Morgan off the market, I felt a definite sense of loss. I would even have sent money to a Save the Morgan fund but for the free rider problem. Do you think that sports car lovers were any less indignant about the Morgan than conservationists would be about Yosemite? Can you prove it? I could claim to be benefited by the fact that the availability of Fords increases my range of choice in cars, even though I have never owned one and probably never will. It certainly is true that production of Fords means the demand for Chevrolets is less than it otherwise would be, hence GM showrooms are less crowded and their prices are lower. I certainly benefit from the production of Ferraris and Maseratis—I don't remember ever seeing one on the street around here, but I have enjoyed looking at some really beautiful photographs. Do all these "external effects" mean that the federal government should subsidize automobile production?

Maybe the external benefits of national parks are quantitatively greater than those that arise from automobile production, organized baseball, or the production of women's clothing. Maybe the external damages of national parks to those who want cheap electricity or cheap lumber, those who enjoy watching movies of lumberjacks and reading stories about miners, and so forth are quantitatively very small. But the burden of quantitative proof lies with the conservationists, and in the absence of such proof no subsidies are justified.

Another form of the organizational argument in favor of national parks is more quickly dealt with. It is sometimes said that conservation groups would be unable to buy the parks because of the sheer organizational difficulty of collecting the money. This objection, I think, is based on the misconception that money would have to be collected door to door in advance of purchase, like American Cancer Society contributions. That is not the case. A group which wanted to buy land for a park would be able to borrow the money from a bank, issue stock or float bonds, guaranteeing repayment out of the fees paid by future visitors. What if this stream of future fees were insufficient to pay back the loan? What would be the justification for the park in the first place if only a few would be willing to pay to use it?

I will concede a point to the organizational argument—that at the ·moment commercial interests do have more ready cash. If all the parks went up for auction tomorrow, the conservationists would be able to bid on very few of them. Consequently, I recommend that the auctioning be done gradually over a period of years, with some of the smaller, less-valuable pieces sold first, to give conservation groups a fair chance to learn the principles of business organization in which commercial interests are already well versed.

Although the public good, irreversibility, and organizational arguments are the conservationists' big guns, there are a number of subsidiary arguments. I will try to deal with these as quickly as possible.

The intergenerational argument states that the wilderness we have now is all we will ever have, so we must pass it on to our children. One generation cannot bind another. We do not have the moral right to deprive our descendants of that which the earth has in limited supply.

This argument would seem to add nothing to the ones already listed. It is in part a variant of the irreversibility doctrine, although that doctrine is even less valid with respect to future generations than to the present. Our sufficiently remote descendants could have, say, all the magnificent groves of four hundred-foot redwoods which we could wish for them, if we just take the trouble to set out the seedlings today. If the wilderness we pass on to our children will be as important to them as to us or even *more* important (something which certainly seems reasonable, given the high income elasticity of demand for outdoor recreation), then they will flock to the parks in more than sufficient numbers with admission fees which will pay the interest on the bonds floated today to reserve those areas for them tomorrow.

Perhaps the most disingenuous argument of all made in favor of our current system of subsidizing national parks out of tax revenue is that this system benefits the poor, who would be excluded by the high fees necessary to cover full costs. The cogency of this argument is seriously weakened by studies which show low-income families to be strongly underrepresented among users of the parks. Far from benefiting the poor, the subsidy to these parks takes taxes collected from the poor, competes in the federal budgetary process with other programs de-signed to aid the poor directly, and uses the money to pay for play-grounds primarily for the well-to-do! As a poverty program the national parks are about on a par with the notorious agricultural subsidies.

The people who support this argument are exhibiting about as enlightened a sense of how to help the poor as Marie Antoinette.[2] If you want to help the poor give them spendable cash grants through a negative income tax, or guaranteed annual income, or whatever you want to call it. Then, if these disadvantaged individuals consider that their first priority is to enjoy the great out-of-doors, they will spend their grants on park admission tickets. If, on the other hand, they consider it more important to buy shoes, good food, a decent apartment—or for that matter, beer, cigarettes, or a new color TV—why should anyone else impose other values on them?

A similar argument dispatches the conservationist defense based on the value of wilderness to science. Not that this value isn't real enough, but if science is to be subsidized, the scientists also should be given unrestricted cash grants. They will spend some of this money on leasing special tracts from private park systems, some more on cyclo-trons, test tubes, and secretarial help. Earmarked grants to science vio-late the equimarginal principle just as do earmarked grants to the poor. If your aim is to help science, why dictate to science the way in which the subsidy must be spent?

Last but not least let's deal with the old line about the spiritual and esthetic values of the wilderness on which you allegedly can't put a price tag. True, the wilderness does have spiritual value for a great many people. In the words of John Muir, founder of the Sierra Club and great prophet of the wilderness:

> Climb the mountains and get their good tidings. Nature's peace will flow into you as sunshine flows into trees. The winds will blow their own freshness into you and the storms their energy, while the cares will drop off like autumn leaves.[3]

But who says that spiritual values must be subsidized by the state; and who says they can't be valued in money? This country has, among its great founding principles, the separation of church and state, based on

---

[2] When faced with the starving French masses, the French queen said, "If they have no bread, let them eat cake!"
[3] Quoted in *Voices for the Wilderness*, William Schwartz, ed. (New York: Ballan-tine Books, Inc., 1969), p. 310.

the belief that nothing is more destructive of spiritual values than put-ting them in the pay of politicians. Do our churches languish because they are financially on their own? No! Men and women everywhere, knowing the importance of spiritual values in their lives, translate these values into cash gifts. No compulsory fees are assessed, yet the free rider problem, so bothersome elsewhere, turns out to be a negligible barrier to the financing of religious organizations. Inspirational literature, books on philosophy and ethics, and spiritual music enjoy brisk sales and gen-erate profits for their producers.

Anyone who claims he has spiritual and esthetic values and won't put his money where is mouth is is putting you on. Anyone who puts his hand in someone else's pocket—someone else who may prefer to get his spiritual experience from Bach or Michelangelo or Elijah Muham-mad—to finance his spiritual uplift is so short on ethics and morality that I would be willing to subsidize a journey for him to a very remote part of the wilderness indeed!

A Positive Program for Preserving the Wilderness

At the beginning of this chapter I said that I place a very high value on the wilderness experience. This, plus a few simple principles of eco-nomics and demography, make me optimistic about the possibilities for preserving the wilderness, provided conservationists develop the will to stand on their own two feet on this issue instead of kneeling in the halls of Congress with their hands out. Here is my four-point program:

1. Absolute top priority goes to the task of getting the govern-ment out of the business of *destroying* the wilderness. The government and its administrative alter egos are wilderness enemy number one—the highway departments, which openly refuse to include scenic values in their cost benefit calculations, but add ridiculously high estimates for equally "intangible" benefits such as the increased comfort of motorists; the Army Corps of Engineers, with their absurd idea of cost-benefit analysis which counts both costs and benefits as benefits;[4] the Depart-ment of Agriculture, which promotes the use of deadly and persistent

[4] Read the literature on the Alaska Ramparts Dam. It will cost a billion and a quarter dollars. The promoters list this as the first benefit, that is, a billion dollars worth of jobs and payroll for the state. Then they add to this the ouput of electricity as a second benefit! On top of that, they refuse to deduct as a cost the value of the wildlife destroyed, and they make their calculations on the basis of a phony below-market rate of interest [see Paul Brooks, "The Plot to Drown Alaska," *The Atlantic Monthly*, May 1965].

pesticides and fertilizers to line the pockets of the already oversubsi-dized farm interests; the AEC, which builds, at the taxpayers' expense, commercially unwarranted "experimental" power stations that release deadly isotopes into the air and pollute our rivers with thermal energy, and which even threatens such horrors as lowering the passes through the Sierras with atom blasts! Then how about the role of government in putting tariffs and quotas on oil, wood products, leather products, meat products, and so forth, thus insuring that the destruction engendered by the production of these items will occur within our own borders rather than abroad? Or how about all the assorted legislators, administrators, and bureaucrats who are in the pocket of offshore drillers, strip miners, sawlog foresters, grazers, prospectors, and dam builders? Next to this incredible list of destructive activities—all of which are financed through the taxes of the same conservationists whose interests they trample upon—the ruination which could be wreaked by private indus-try unaided pales in comparison. Fortunately, conservation groups are already hard at work on this first-priority assignment.

2.   The next part of the plan is of almost equal priority—get the government out of the business of *protecting* the wilderness. As was already emphasized in the discussion of irreversibility, when the last shreds of the most beautiful scenery in the world are at stake, conserva-tionists should want the decision-making powers firmly in their own grip and not in the fickle hands of any committee or agency in Washington. Only when the wilderness belongs to the conservationists will it be safe.

3.   In order to be ready to take over when objectives 1. and 2. have been accomplished, the third high-priority task is to begin a crash program to convert the wilderness passion which spills forth so freely as a stream of words into an equally abundant stream of dollars. Money talks, and conservationists, unless they are just play acting when they say how much they value their parks, have tremendous potential re-sources to tap. I am not a specialist in these matters, but I can offer some common-sense suggestions as illustrations of what is possible.

Most important, put an immediate end to queuing as a means of rationing space in recreational facilities which are already overcrowded. When a definite level of capacity can be defined—and this applies to most campsites, for example—charge admission fees high enough to limit applications to available space. This means varying the rate over the course of the season. I can imagine certain key spots where a camp-ground might be filled on Labor Day or the Fourth of July with each camper gladly putting up $100.00. (After all, people already pay prices like this for scalped tickets to the World Series or the Superbowl.) The less wealthy or enthusiastic, and those fortunates who have a more flexible work schedule, will be able to gain admission to the sites for much lower fees on week-days and in off-peak seasons. Waiting in line represents the least efficient, least just, and most easily corrupted form of rationing ever devised. It could be eliminated even while the parks are still government-owned, if conservationists would only have the honesty to tell the park administrators that they are ready to pay their own way and stop trying to take a free ride.

A second useful financial mechanism is the practice of "excess taking," frequently used in New England to finance such establishments as ski slopes. If you want 1000 acres to build a ski run, you buy that 1000 acres and the adjoining 1000 acres. As soon as the facility is built, the surrounding land is sold off at several times its purchase price as homesites and commercial properties to those who are attracted to the area by the available recreation. Conservationists have spent much time fulminating against speculators and developers, yet isn't it obvious that wherever a park is built, land values will inevitably go up and speculative profits will be made? So why not get a piece of the action and put these profits to work in a good cause?

The prospects for raising money by both of these methods are greatly enhanced by what might be called Udall's laws after the former Secretary of the Interior who attached great importance to them. Udall's first law: The available open land per capita decreases more than in proportion to the increase in population. (Take 4000 open acres, 1000 people, 1000 residential and commercial acres, 4 open acres per person. Double the population, develop another 1000 acres for commercial and residential use, and you are left with 2000 people and 3000 open acres, 1-1/2 acres per person.) Udall's second law: The demand for outdoor recreation increases faster than in proportion to the increase of GNP per capita.

Take these two laws together and it may be true, for example, that a doubling of the population of an area could increase the demand for outdoor recreation by a factor of nine or ten! Translated into dollars and cents, Udall's laws mean that you are never going to have to worry about demand for your product or how to pay off those wilderness development bonds.

There is also much money to be raised by such methods as

conservation window stickers and private philanthropy. By the time the parks go up for auction, the money could be there to buy them, *if* plans are laid now.

4.   The fourth point of the program is to get the conservationists down out of the rarefied air of the high Sierras and develop in them a realistic attitude toward outdoor recreation areas of the nonvirgin, non-wilderness variety. As a Secretary of the Interior once put it, the whole question of recreation is analogous to a flood control project. If you let all the masses of people flow into the parks in an uncontrolled fashion, then a great deal of damage will be done. But if upstream, along the watersheds of the cities and highways, you install control works, diversions, overflow areas, holding reservoirs, and so forth, then the flood can be controlled when it reaches true wilderness areas.

Such a program means buying low-grade, unspectacular, logged-over, or cropped-over areas, especially in the Eastern and Midwestern sections of the country, and restoring them to provide maximum recreational potential. Low-grade wilderness surrogates like these, if properly located and properly developed and managed, can protect the remaining virgin wilderness in two ways, both by the flood control function already mentioned and by producing revenue which can be used to maintain the low-use, high-grade havens of the purists elsewhere.

chapter 8

TOWARD AN ECOLOGICALLY VIABLE ECONOMY

We began this book by drawing the distinction between the myth of the throughput economy and the reality of spaceship earth. Throughout the intervening chapters we have continually reiterated the theme that as long as our economic system is adapted to the myth and not to the reality of the world we live in, we are in trouble. Even if the human race is lucky enough to escape the worst prophecies of gloom and doom—extinction via nuclear war, massive flooding, a new ice age, or the teretogenic effects of pesticides and herbicides—we are still faced with the inevitable prospect that our throughput economy will simply run out of usable sources and sinks, and that we will have to spend an ever-greater fraction of our Gross National Product cleaning up after ourselves.

So far we have largely confined ourselves to what economists call the microeconomic point of view, that is, to detailed consideration of the ways in which the decision-making context of individual consumers, enterprises, and interest groups could be altered to provide incentives for the avoidance of ecologically destructive activities. Now we will take a brief look at some macroeconomic aspects of the spaceship earth economy which we will sooner or later have to establish, which is to say, we will back off and try to see the problem as a whole.

There was a period during the first years of the last decade when in the economics departments of our great universities the most popular topic in macroeconomics was economic growth. With the inauguration of President John Kennedy it seemed that the Keynesian revolution had been completed and that the problems of economic stability, inflation, and unemployment, which had preoccupied macroeconomics since the thirties, would be banished once and for all. At this juncture the young avant-garde economists turned their attention to the promotion of economic growth as the great panacea which would conquer the next set of problems—poverty, underdevelopment, and catching up with the Russians.

Suddenly the era of growthmanship is over. Today the Young Turks of the economics profession are increasingly questioning the necessity and desirability of economic growth. Many of them would even go as far as the editors of *Ramparts,* who write that "we simply don't need any more Gross National Product, any more unnecessary goods and factories. What we do need is a *redistribution* of existing real wealth, and a *reallocation* of society's resources." [1] The ecologically concerned, it seems, view the abandonment of economic growth as one of those "painful self-sacrifices" that we are called upon to make.

Is there anything of substance to this new wave of antigrowthmanship? Yes, there is. As the reader is already aware, to the extent that the goal of growth meant growth of Type II GNP, a grossly misleading measure of human welfare, it was an unworthy goal. And to the extent that each individual microeconomic unit of the economy grew by imposing an increasing fraction of the costs of growth on outsiders, economic expansion meant the growth of inefficiency and waste along with the growth of output. Still, the conclusion sometimes advanced by ecological radicals that we must limit ourselves to a *steady state* economy

---

Ramparts, May 1970, p. 4. Italics in original.

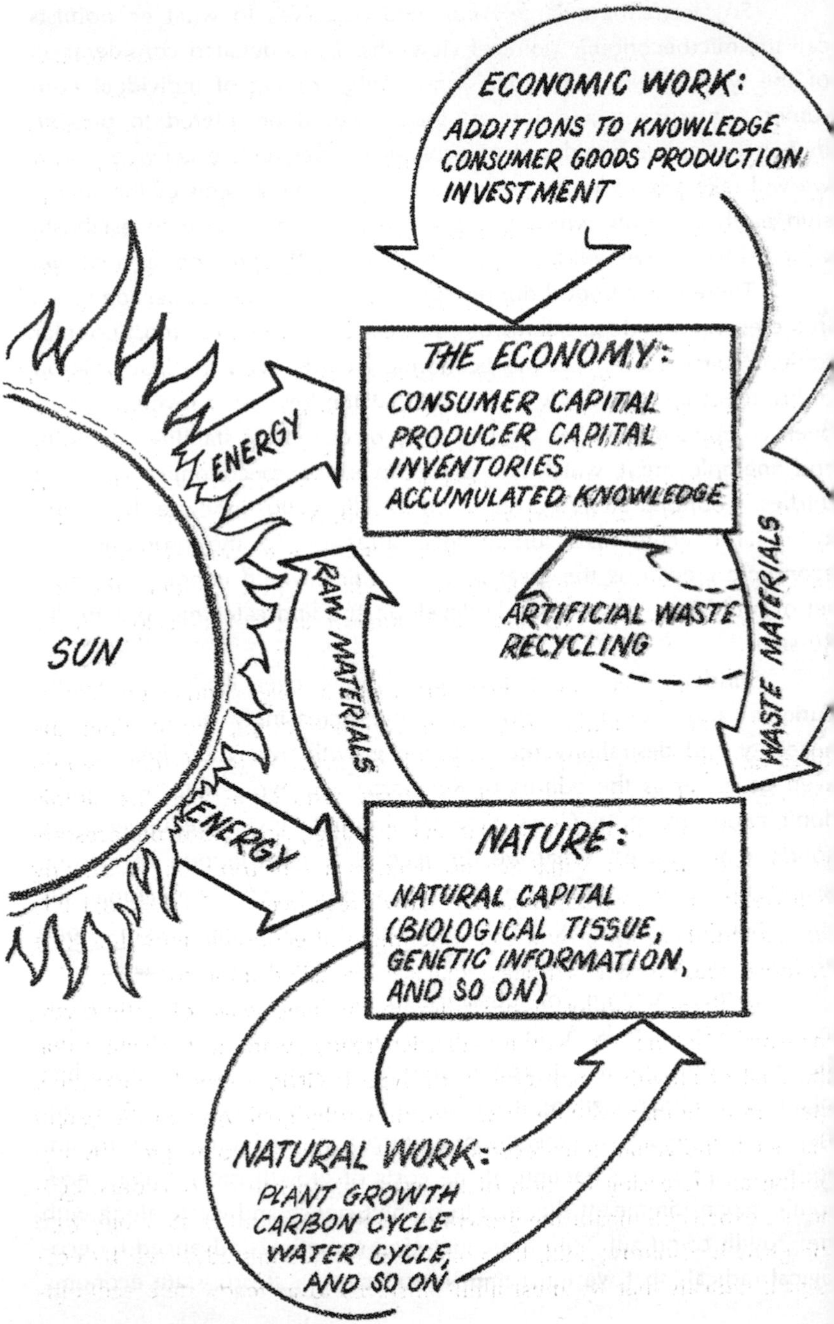

FIGURE 8.1 Detailed view of the spaceship earth

eschewing *all* economic growth is, I think, unwarranted. To understand why this is so we must look a bit more closely at the mechanics of our spaceship earth.

Figure 8.1 shows the same spaceship earth model as Figure 1.2, this time with the skin stripped away to allow for greater detail. The basic components of this diagram are again the two boxes labeled "the economy," and "nature." (Let's agree not to split hairs about what goes in which box in certain marginal cases like agriculture, forestry, or fishing.) These two boxes are really much more alike in function than you might guess. Each of them is filled with "capital," a substance which we may think of very broadly as lumps of matter and encoded information capable of allowing work to be performed. The capital in the economy consists of producer capital (machinery, buildings, instruments, and so forth), consumer capital (cars, refrigerators, clothing), accumulated human knowledge (sometimes called "human capital"), and inventories of things like bread and gasoline. Nature also has a capital stock, which consists of such things as the organized body tissues of living plants and animals, the stock of genetically coded information of how to replicate the first component, and certain "natural inventories" like coal deposits and water in high mountain lakes. You could also include such things as the hoards of nuts stashed away by the world's squirrel population.

The existence of capital in both the natural and economic realms makes possible the performance of *work*. Economic and biologic subsystems are endowed with the ability to tap certain energy sources and apply the energy to the process of taking up available raw materials and changing their chemical, physical, or locational properties. Whether this takes place on an automobile assembly line or through the process of plant growth, some work is performed while producing useful products, and some waste is generated in the form of products useless to the unit in question.

The concept of *entropy*, if physicists will permit a loose borrowing, is very helpful in understanding the operation of natural and economic systems as working, energy transducing, waste eliminating mechanisms. Entropy, in the broad sense in which we will use the term, means randomness or disorder. The concept of entropy can be easily illustrated with a deck of cards. Build a card house six or seven stories high, and you have a system of low entropy. Knock the house over and you get a random pile of cards on the floor, a system of much higher entropy.

In accordance with the TANSTAAFL principle, it requires an input of energy to reduce the entropy of a system (building the card house). Conversely, a system may release energy in the process of changing over to a state of increased entropy (the card house falling down).

Entropy is of interest to the economist because the goal of all man's economic activity, generally speaking, is to reduce the entropy of his immediate surroundings. (Kenneth Boulding speaks of an "entropy theory of value.") Man builds houses, writes books, weaves clothing, organizes sports events, and so on—all of which represent systems of relatively reduced entropy. Items of reduced entropy are "goods," but in their production certain other items of increased entropy—"bads"— must also be produced. These are waste products. Just as man tries to keep the low entropy goods close to him; he tries to put the high entropy bads as far out of sight as possible.

The only possible case of when man's productive energies are consciously devoted to the *increase* of entropy is in that peculiar activity called warfare. This may be "the exception which proves the rule," for even in warfare men try to keep the zones of entropy increase as far from their home base as possible.

Now we are equipped to raise the interesting question, what happens to the total entropy within each of our two little boxes, nature and the economy, over time? Let's begin before man came upon the scene. Nature was hard at work for millennia transducing the energy of the sun and creating highly ordered biological systems on the surface of the earth. More and more complex forms of life were evolved and multiplied. Coal beds were laid down. Towering forests sprang up. More and more elaborate libraries of genetic information were painstakingly accumulated.

Enter man. At first, he was part of nature and his appearance counted as a further reduction of the entropy of the natural system. At some point he began to engage in something which we can legitimately call economic activity, and from then on he busied himself for generation after generation with the creation of ever greater and grander low economic entropy zones in the form of artifacts, cities, cultures, and civilizations. Since early man was not able to utilize the rays of the sun directly, he tapped earthly nature for both raw materials and energy sources. Each step in the reduction of economic entropy was made at the expense of an increase in the entropy of nature. This started as soon as men began burning sticks to heat their caves. But for a long time man's economic activities appeared as only the tiniest blip on the fringes of the natural world. Despite the small entropy increase suffered at the hand of man, nature continued to photosynthesize, to evapotranspirate, and to nibble away at the net entropy of the earth's surface.

Eventually the Industrial Revolution came along. Man spread over the whole surface of the globe and multiplied at a fanstastic exponential rate. Enormous tracts of forest were cut down; colossal mountains of iron ore were smelted; vast pools of oil and beds of coal were extracted and their molecules converted into high entropy carbon dioxide with the release of stored energy. At some point, man's ability to reduce economic entropy at nature's expense began to exceed the ability of nature to reduce its own entropy at the sun's expense. (Have you noticed that all of what we have described goes on ultimately at the expense of the sun, which gains entropy every second and will eventually burn down to a cosmic clinker, putting an end, in a few billion more years, to nature and the economy alike?)

That is the phase in which we find ourselves at present. The economy is growing; economic capital is increasing; economic entropy is being reduced; but, in exchange, natural capital is being run down faster than it can be replaced; and natural entropy is rising to the danger point. This can be seen quite clearly in the phenomenon of the rising carbon dioxide content of the atmosphere to which we have already alluded.

It is this destructive aspect of economic growth which worries the antigrowthmen, the ecologists, and the conservationists. Let's stop exploiting nature, they say, and pass what's left of our environment on to our descendents in at least no worse a condition than when we found it. Let's establish a closed-circuit economy which dumps no more high entropy waste products into our environment than can be converted by natural processes back into useful substances. Can this be done and, if so, what are its implications for economic growth?

The answer to this double question depends partly on technology. If we had to limit production of wastes to those of a quantity and quality which could be handled by purely natural cycles, we would have to undergo a *very* sharp reduction in production of useful output. Fortunately, artificial cycles to supplement the natural ones are possible. Although our current methods of artificially recycling waste products are primitive (even in those cases where we do recycle waste—as in the production of steel from scrap—the recycling process itself often produces waste products of its own) this area of technology is growing very rapidly.

Ecologists and conservationists are extremely suspicious of technology and the purported ability of technology to save the world. This
suspicion is justified by the careless and destructive application of
technology by gung-ho engineers and by the glib claims of certain
overly complacent souls that technology can repair any damage which
technology might inadvertently cause. Yet unless the world is to return
to a hunting and gathering society of a few hundred thousand individuals (this is just what certain people with whom I have talked
desire) a closed-circuit economy cannot be established without the
aid of technology, and in particular that of waste recycling.

But technology alone is not enough. Waste recycling requires
organization, and organization requires financing. Who is going to
provide the organization and financing of waste recycling, assuming
that the necessary technology can be developed? In answer to this
question, here are a few passages from Jane Jacobs' excellent book,
The Economy of Cities:

> One of the oldest forms of waste recycling is the reprocessing
> of waste paper. One producer of book paper advertises that its
> papers are more resistant to deterioration from humidity and
> temperature changes than paper made from new pulp [I hope
> this book is being printed on the stuff—E.G.D.], and accompanies
> these advertisements with striking photographs of New York City,
> which it calls its "concrete forests." This fancy, that the city is
> another kind of paperyielding forest, is rather apt; but the met-
> aphor of the waste-yielding mine may be more comprehensive.
> For in the highly developed economies of the future, it is
> probable that cities will become huge, rich, and diverse mines
> of raw materials. These mines will differ from any now to be
> found because they will become richer the more and longer they
> are exploited. The law of diminishing returns applies to other
> mining operations: the richest veins, having been worked out,
> are gone forever. But in the cities, the same materials will be
> retrieved over and over again. . . . The largest, most prosperous
> cities will be the richest, the most easily worked, and the most
> inexhaustible mines. . . .
>
> How will the mines be organized? . . . A type of work that
> does not now exist [will be] necessary: services that collect
> wastes, not for shunting into incinerators or gulches, but for
> distributing to various primary specialists from whom the materi-
> als will go to converters or reusers. The comprehensive collect-
> ing services, as they develop into big businesses, will use many

technical devices. They will install and service equipment for collecting sulfuric acid, soot, fly ash, and other wastes in fuel stacks, including gasses that, at present, cannot be trapped. They will supply and handle containers for containerized wastes and will install fixed equipment such as chutes, probably by employing subcontractors. Who will develop the comprehensive collecting services? My guess is that the work, when it does appear, will be added on to janitorial contracting services. . . .

Comprehensive collectors of wastes may at first derive their incomes like the St. Petersburg trash and garbage processing plant which gets a $3 fee per ton for handling wastes and derives the rest of its income from the sale of its products. Just so, comprehensive waste collectors may at first be paid fees—either directly by those whose wastes they collect, or indirectly by them through taxes, or by a combination of both. This will cover the services of handling wastes not yet convertible or valuable for reuse. But they will also derive income from the wastes they do pass on. As proportions of unused wastes become smaller and the income derived from sales becomes larger, comprehensive collectors will compete for the privilege of doing the collecting work free, just as some collectors of profitable special wastes do now. Eventually they will compete for collection rights by offering fees for waste concessions, again just as some collectors of special wastes now do. In large cities, the comprehensive collectors will handle and distribute annually many, many millions of tons of materials and will supply immense numbers and varieties of converter industries and recyclers of special wastes.[2]

What stands between us and Jane Jacobs' future city-mines? A few technological refinements, yes. But technology is not something which just happens; technology is developed largely on demand to service the most profitable and rapidly expanding sectors of industry. Waste recycling would be no exception. What really stands between us and commercially profitable waste recycling is the fact that the government now subsidizes primitive throughput-type waste disposal systems. The subsidy takes the form of city dumps and free or below cost rubbish removal. It also takes the form of public ownership of water resources, into which liquid wastes are dumped without the imposition of user fees. And, in addition, the subsidy takes the form of obsolete provisions in our legal system which allow you to dump your

Jane Jacobs, The Economy of Cities (N.Y.: Random House, Inc., 1969).

waste into my airspace without threat of a suit from me for the violation of my property rights. If this unfair, inefficient, and ecologically
destructive competition were taken away we would *already* be in phase
one of the development of commercial waste recycling (the phase
where waste producers pay a fee to have waste removed), even with
our *present* technology. Starting from that point things would soon
develop until the flow of artificially recycled waste products back into
the economy (shown in Figure 8.1 by the broken arrow) would grow
from a trickle into a torrent, which would dwarf the input of raw
materials taken from natural sources.

In this way we could eventually settle our entropy balance with
the environment. We could adjust the waste-resource cycle so that we
passed the environment on to our heirs in just the state we found it
or, better yet, we could actually put less than the maximum burden
on the regenerative powers of nature and pass it on in an improved
form!

Commercial waste recycling will mean increased cost for the
producers of many products, and some of these costs will be passed on
to consumers as price increases. It will get pretty expensive to maintain
such luxuries as aluminum beer cans, no-return bottles, disposable
diapers, and jar-inside-a-box-inside-another-box packaging when these
gimmicks are no longer implicitly subsidized as they are now. We can
imagine that the makers of some of these products will go out of
business or, better, diversify into waste recycling or the production of
biodegradable wrapping materials.

While the natural world kept on an even keel in this future,
or was gradually allowed to regenerate, economic growth would continue inside the box called the economy, fueled by a constant input
of solar energy (perhaps fusion energy too—I don't know much about
the environmental implications of this) and a constant accumulation
of knowledge. Assuming that the population problem is controlled,
life within this zone of reduced entropy would become more and more
pleasant. Many people would take the fruits of this growth in the form
of increased leisure; others in the form of increased consumption of
artifacts and services. As long as the latter are all produced out of
"clean" Type I GNP, even the old conflict about which of these alternatives is the path to the good life would be laid to rest.

In this ultimate closed-circuit economy of the future a great
many sources of social conflict would be absent. With more people

aying their own ways and fewer living on tax-financed handouts, there would be less reason for the donor to dictate the behavior of the recipient. With lower taxes the level of political tension would be reduced and civil tranquility would be promoted. And with an economy which was not based on the transfer of raw materials from the poor nations to the rich, prospects for establishing peace through the world rule of law would be much improved.

One degree of freedom still remains in our model, an important detail which must be specified before the model is complete. The astute reader (the same one who has been one jump ahead of me all the way through the book), will have guessed what this is. Although we have specified that the economy of the future will eventually adjust to the spaceshiplike closed-loop reality of relationship to the natural environment, this adjustment could be made at any of a wide range of possible levels.

It has already been suggested that the primitive hunting and gathering economy of our neolithic ancestors satisfied the specification that they took from nature no more for entropy reduction and returned to it no more in waste than could be restored by natural processes. At the other extreme this condition might also be satisfied by a purely artificial economy on a totally sterile globe. Robert Heinlein describes just such an economy in *The Moon Is a Harsh Mistress*. The setting is a colony on the moon which, threatened with a cut-off of all imports from earth, has to develop a total economic recycling process for every material used. Nature gives no help at all except in such details as maintaining the carbon cycle with the aid of plants grown under artificial light in synthetic soil with artificially recycled water. All this is written with reference to the moon, but the surface of the earth, according to some of the gloomier (but not to be entirely discounted) predictions, will eventually come close to resembling this state if we don't quit abusing it.

Will we rid ourselves of the throughput myth only at that ultimate point when the nature box of our model has been squeezed absolutely dead and dry? Must we revert to a neolithic level of existence to avoid this fate? Obviously, the answer is no on both counts. We can stop the deterioration of the environment and settle our entropy balance with nature at any given point whatsoever along the route between these two extremes. The choice is ours.

How shall we choose? Shall we leave it to the Department of

Agriculture, the Department of the Interior, or some new-fangled Central Environmental Administration? Shall we take the matter out of the hands of the bureaucrats and turn it over to the legislature, where our elected representatives sit in air-conditioned comfort dividing up the pork? Shall we, perhaps, hold a new constitutional convention on the two hundredth anniversary of 1789, and pass an environmental bill of rights? Or shall we leave the decision up to free men to make for themselves, casting their votes in that most democratic of all forums, the market place?

The reader should have no doubt about which one of these alternatives I am about to recommend. This ultimate macroeconomic decision must be made in the market place, just as all the micro-economic decisions to which we have devoted previous chapters should be. The result would be something like the following.

First, remember that the market can be relied upon to make an efficient decision (one which involves no unnecessary waste or missed opportunities), a just decision (one which involves no violation of the human rights or property rights of any participant), and an equitable decision (one which respects the principle of to each according to his work) only when each man in his every act of production and consumption bears the FULL COST of his actions. How to fine tune the market system to accomplish this end has been the subject of most of this book.

If, tomorrow morning say, everyone in the world started paying his own way, it must be obvious that a great many abuses of the environment would stop. The airlines could never hope to pay off all those suits against the sonic boom, so the SST would be scrapped. Motorists would have to start paying emission charges, and would convert their machines to natural gas or electricity, if they didn't switch to the railroad. Lumbermen would be confined to farming their tree farms. All this would happen very quickly.

It wouldn't take long before commercial recycling firms were set up to mine all those smokestacks, sewers, and garbage heaps. Eventually, as people were made to bear the full costs of having children, and as they learned the full benefits of small families, the population would level off or even gently decline. Within a few years most of the flows in and out of the nature box of Figure 8.1 would taper off to an equilibruim level.

In other areas I think we would and should continue to tap certain types of irreplaceable resources as long as they last. I see no

ong reason, for example, for not pumping out pretty much all of the
orld's deposits of oil and gas. Eventually, exploitation of these re-
urces would cease when the costs of extraction (remember that these
ould be somewhat increased, since firms would have to take greater
ecautions about leakages and spillages, and because their depletion
owance tax loophole would be closed) caught up with the price for
nich the products could be sold. The mining of many metals and
nerals would probably also continue for a long time. Under a full
st system things like strip mining of coal would immediately become
losing proposition, but we would probably get pretty much all of
e world's supply of lead and tin out of the ground before we were
ally reduced to using nothing but reprocessed scrap. The extraction
things like sand and clay might go on almost indefinitely.

All of these continuing extractive activities would help make the
orld a better place in which to live. While they continued, they would
lp ease the sharp rise in the cost of living which would occur initially,
fore Type I GNP caught up with the current level of combined Type
nd Type II. And even after they ultimately stopped, the total stock
metals and minerals kept in circulation by the recycling firms would
larger. In no case could these extractive activities continue at a profit
nere the costs—internal and external, commercial, esthetic and eco-
gical—outweighed these obvious benefits.

While in some respects the natural environment remained much
it is now, and in some was further depleted, in other very important
ays the environment would be improved and restored. Foremost
nong the areas of restoration would be those "great natural sewers"
North America. It might be predicted that within two years after
r program began, Wall Street executives would be entertaining their
ents at a Hudson River Swimming Club. Even Lake Erie might revive.
e air would be cleaner than before, and the cities quieter. If ecology
partments in our colleges begin to offer a few courses in business
ong with science, the areas of wilderness available for recreation
ould increase.

In short, the world would eventually approach an equilibrium,
e in which most of that which we have today would be preserved
t with cleaner air and water above and emptier wells and mines
low. We can get there, if we get the government out of the business
environmental destruction and let the market teach us that great
ological principle: "There Ain't No Such Thing as A Free Lunch!"

BIBLIOGRAPHICAL NOTE AND SUGGESTIONS FOR FURTHER READING

order not to clutter the text, footnotes have for the most part been
d to give credit for specific citations. As many readers will have
ticed, however, I have at several points rather freely adapted ideas
m a variety of sources. By listing some of these here, I hope not
ly to give credit where credit is due but to suggest directions for
ther reading for those whose interest has been aroused, or for those
o seek material with which to rebut some of my more controversial
inions.

The basic contrast between the throughput and spaceship models
the economy introduced in the first chapter is primarily inspired
Kenneth Boulding. The reader might be particularly interested in

looking at the section on ecology in *Economics as a Science* (New York: McGraw-Hill, Inc., 1970), and also at his excellent article in *The Environmental Crisis*, ed., Harold W. Helfrich, Jr. (New Haven, Conn.: Yale University Press, 1970). Robert Heilbroner has also been a leader in the campaign to urge ecological thinking upon economists, for example, by renaming GNP Gross National Cost.

I adapted pollution control suggestions made by a variety of writers in Chapter 3. For an elaboration of the program for auto exhaust emission the reader is referred to an article by Larry E. Ruff entitled "The Economic Common Sense of Pollution" in *The Public Interest*, No. 19 (Spring 1970). Some ideas for creating property rights to protect waterways from pollution have been advanced by J.H. Dales in his book, *Pollution, Property, and Prices* (Toronto: University of Toronto Press, 1968). Frank Bubb has written on pollution and the law of nuisance in *The Libertarian Forum*, Vol. II, No. 8 (April 15, 1970).

In recent years a great deal of interesting literature has appeared on the subject of public choice and collective action. I found Mancur Olsen's *The Logic of Collective Action* (Cambridge, Mass.: The Harvard University Press, 1965) to be particularly useful in preparing part of Chapter 4. My thoughts in this area have been even more strongly influenced by James Buchanan and Gordon Tullock's classic, *Calculus of Consent* (Ann Arbor, Mich.: University of Michigan Press, 1962). A more recent but much more technical work by Buchanan, *The Demand and Supply of Public Goods* (Skokie, Ill.: Rand McNally & Company, 1968) goes into certain issues in more detail.

On the subject of population I would like again to recommend the "collage of controversial ideas" assembled by Garrett Hardin in *Population, Evolution, and Birth Control*, 2nd ed. (San Francisco: W.H. Freeman and Company, 1969). After working through that the reader will have many ideas on where to get further information. For those who prefer to get their economics in the form of fiction I would suggest *Stand on Zanzibar* by John Brunner (New York: Ballentine Books, Inc., 1968), a novel about the population explosion.

I encountered some difficulty in finding a systematic exposition of ecological considerations in economic development. Paul and Anne Ehrlich discuss some of the problems involved in *Population, Resources, and Environment*. (San Francisco: W.H. Freeman and Co., 1970). At a late stage in writing, I had a brief opportunity to examine an advance copy of John Culbertson's *Economic Development and Ecological Approach*

(New York: Alfred A. Knopf, 1971), which I think will go a long way toward filling this gap.

If the reader wishes to give the conservationists a fair chance to state their own case, I recommend *Voices for the Wilderness,* William Schwartz, ed. (New York: Ballentine Books, Inc., 1969). I drew much of the material for Chapter 7 from this source, I hope without excessive distortion.